Addiction, Procrastination, and Laziness:

A Proactive Guide to the Psychology of Motivation

D1114018

By Roman Gelperin

Addiction, Procrastination, and Laziness: A Proactive Guide to the Psychology of Motivation (second edition), by Roman Gelperin

Visit the author's website at: www.RomanGelperin.com

ISBN: 9781549786150

Table of Contents

Introduction

I wrote this short book back in 2013, after beating my head painfully, persistently against the thick wall of my motivational problems, and finally breaking out into full understanding, acceptance, and self-control. I dealt with these issues the same way I deal, and recommend dealing, with all psychological troubles: through introspection—that is, by paying attention to the subtle workings of one's own mind, identifying the roots of the problem, and devising the corresponding solution.

I wrote this book as a type of self-help manual, targeting the most common motivational problems in the world today, against which most people end up wrecking themselves, but that can be easily and effectively solved by a correct understanding of their own minds. Other than quitting cigarettes, I intimately experienced all the motivational problems described in this book.

The five examples in Chapter One are of composite persons: based on my own personal introspections, and on my extensive observations of the people around me, who I saw struggling with the same issues. As for the smoking example, I was never addicted to cigarettes, and therefore never needed to quit. But from my countless observations of smokers around me—attempting, usually failing, and once again trying to quit—I noticed their quandary had the same essential determinants as every other motivational problem, and could therefore be solved using the same methods.

Since writing this book, I've applied every technique I advocate in it to my own life, and with amazing success. I only hope the hard-won insights I lay out on its pages will prove as useful to you, as they have been for me.

Chapter 1

Anomalies in Human Behavior

Over the course of our lives, we have all no doubt had a chance to observe certain anomalies in our own behavior. And I do not mean this in the sense of the overstated fact, so often gaudily proclaimed by psychology students and enthusiasts, that *"human beings behave irrationally."* What they refer to hardly manages to scratch the surface of the archaic psychic mechanisms that are at play in the human mind.

It isn't simply that people behave or even think "irrationally," but that the conscious control we exert over our behavior has sometimes partial, sometimes little, and sometimes no bearing on our manifest actions. For anyone who has paid this any due attention, it is indeed hard not to get the impression that some antagonistic forces within us are constantly pushing, pulling, and determining our actions, no matter what our conscious intentions are, and in spite of any deliberate opposition we may put up. Nearly all self-observant persons will concede that they are not in full control of their behavior. And there are many who feel that they truly have no control at all. In large part, they are correct.

Procrastination

It has been six weeks since Jim was assigned an eight-page

paper for his American Literature class. He had thought about it frequently over the elapsed time. He concluded that it would take no more than ten total hours to complete it. He had multiple times made a resolution to begin the paper, planning to get it out of the way early. He shunned those resolutions over and over again, and hasn't as much as written a word of it. Only now, in the dead of night, exactly ten hours before it is due, Jim begins feverishly writing and cobbling words together. Every minute of the next ten hours Jim spends intensely working, taking no breaks to rest, watch television, or play videogames, as he is usually prone to doing. He feels stressed, irritated, exhausted, but in the course of those ten hours he manages to complete the paper and hands it in right on time.

Now Jim feels elated. He feels a huge relief, a grand weight lifted off his shoulders, he is ecstatic, he no longer feels tired despite staying up the extra ten hours to write the paper. He thinks he can tackle anything, overcome any hurdle. "Never again," he thinks, "from now on I will never leave an assignment to the last minute and have to spend such an excruciating time rushing to complete it." But, of course, Jim is doomed to find himself repeating this process over and over again; procrastinating for days, and weeks, and months before beginning his assignments; and always waiting until the very last minute before his assignment is due, and when stalling any longer would cause him to flunk it.[1]

Without a doubt this is an extremely common scenario, one which many of us have experienced at one time or another, if not perpetually so. So why does it happen? Why do we waste countless hours on unproductive, frivolous activities,

---

[1] This example, and the four that follow it, are composites of real people in real situations. Except for example three, they were drawn from my own personal experience, and from my observations of the people around me dealing with the same problems. Only example three, about smoking, is based primarily on my observations of other people, and—only secondarily—on a few analogous experiences of my own.

when we know there's work to be done? Why can't so many of us resist the urge to procrastinate? What separates those of us who do, from those who diligently complete all their work early or in a timely fashion? Why can't we force ourselves to work, even though we know it isn't worth the stress and anxiety that we will experience in rushing to do it at the last second? And, of course, the work itself then suffers on top of that. Many will conclude that they just have "no willpower." And yet, in those final moments right before the assignment is due, the "willpower" we call up to do it is nothing short of incredible. At those times we may feel that if only we could harness that motivation, we would be capable of anything. But no one would wish onto themselves the constant, feverish pressure of continuously having to complete a task under this type of hard deadline. And those whose job puts them in these kinds of conditions most often greatly resent it. There can, of course, be many negative physical and psychological side-effects as well.

It is, however, possible to have the best of both worlds: to be productive and proactive without the stress and strain that comes with having to meet a deadline. And it has little to do with *willpower;* as we will soon see, willpower is only a skittish and insignificant factor. What it requires is an understanding of motivation. But let's leave this issue hanging for now and take in a few more examples.

Loss of Motivation

Annemarie is trying to lose weight. She buys a membership to a local gym, and for the first two weeks she goes there eagerly every day and gets an admirable workout. On the first day of the third week she feels a reluctance to go, but she still manages to pick herself up and visits the gym anyway. The day after that she decides that it would be OK to skip a day, and doesn't go. And from that point forward, just as with so many people, she begins having an extremely hard time bringing herself to visit the gym. Most days she is unable to overcome this dreadful feeling and ends up failing to go at all. Soon she finds herself only going to the gym once a week, then once every two weeks, and eventually she stops going altogether.

This is, of course, a typical case of loss of motivation, and an incredibly common one today.

Cigarette Addiction

John is 36 years old. He works at an accounting firm, and is trying to quit cigarettes, a habit he's been maintaining for the past 18 years. He smokes half a pack a day, but decides to quit cold-turkey. At many instances throughout his day, he has a strong urge for a cigarette, but then he remembers his vow to quit, and resists it. The first day he succeeds in resisting his urges and doesn't smoke even a single cigarette. The next day, however, upon walking home from work, he is surprised to find that a lit cigarette has found its way into his mouth, and that he is happily puffing away at it.

He had taken a pack out of his pocket, extracted a cigarette from it, put it into his mouth, pulled a lighter from his pocket, lit the cigarette, replaced both the pack and the lighter into his pocket once more, and only after taking several large puffs from it does he realize that he's just done all this, and actively defied his vow to quit smoking. He takes one last deep drag from the cigarette and throws it out.

The next day, to prevent a reoccurrence of this, he takes the pack out of his pocket and stores it in his desk drawer at work. He frequently yearns to have a smoke, but then he imagines having to reach into the drawer to get it and stops himself. Soon enough, however, he finds himself outside with the pack in his hand and a lit cigarette in his mouth. He retrieved it from the drawer, went outside and deliberately lit the cigarette. He was conscious of his actions, but only after taking a few puffs of the cigarette does he realize his guilt: grasping the full consequence of failing to uphold his vow against smoking. He throws the cigarette out violently.

On the next day, he throws out his pack altogether in order

to not even have the opportunity to reach for it. Once again, his urges to smoke are powerful, but he has no ready opportunity to indulge them, so he abstains. Over the course of the day, however, he discovers that he has made very little progress in his work and that his thoughts were being constantly drawn from his job to the act of going to the grocery store to buy a pack of cigarettes. He finally decides that this painful attempt to quit is having unacceptable consequences for his professional life. He goes to the store to buy a new pack, deciding to put off his attempt to quit smoking for a later time—perhaps when he takes a vacation. John goes back to his regular routine of smoking half a pack a day.

In this example, John actually put up quite a valiant effort to quit his addiction; a much better effort than most people put up when they try to quit smoking. But, alas, he was missing one crucial component in his strategy to quit cigarettes. We'll see by the end of this book whether we can give John some advice on how, next time, to quit successfully.

Videogame Addiction

Junseo is home from college on winter break. He has a moderate amount of homework and a few personal things he wants to accomplish while he is at home, but nothing urgent. On his first day home he wakes up at eight in the morning. The rest of his family is asleep and he has no desire to go anywhere. He is bored. To quell his boredom Junseo decides to indulge in a frequent childhood pastime of his and play a videogame. He hasn't played any videogames whatsoever in a long time, and he never had the slightest inclination to do so in college. The PlayStation 2 he owned since childhood is still in his room, and he slides in an old game he had completely forgotten about. He starts the game anew, having a slight feeling of nostalgia, and for the next couple of hours he spends an enjoyable time reacquainting himself with its workings.

At ten o'clock he has breakfast. Finding himself full and rather lethargic, he ascertains that there still isn't anything substantial for him to do, and he returns again to the video-game. For several more hours he plays the game and is still somewhat entertained by it. He looks at the clock and sees that it's 1:30 PM. "It's about time to quit this and go about my day," he thinks; "I should go for a jog, get my homework out of the way early, maybe see some old friends." He gets ready to leave the house but then decides to play for 15 more minutes before doing so. Those fifteen minutes pass, but he still feels unsatisfied, and decides to give himself another 10 minutes. He does this perpetually, sometimes losing track of time, and granting himself a ten-minute extension whenever he realizes he has played long past his self-imposed quota. Only at 5 PM, when he becomes very hungry, is he able to quit the game and finally leave his house.

He decides to go for a jog and eat a hamburger at a local restaurant. He does so. But when he gets home, he cannot bring himself to do any homework and defaults once again to the videogame. He plays the game uninterrupted well into the night and only abandons it at 2 AM when he is utterly exhausted. He falls asleep.

The next day he wakes up at 10:30 AM, breakfasts, and feels a strong urge to once again indulge in the videogame. He made plans that day to meet with a couple friends around 7 PM at a bar. He decides it'd be OK to play the game for a bit, since there is still so much time until the arranged meeting. Callous to the passage of time, he plays the videogame for eight straight hours. At exactly seven o'clock he remembers that he must meet his friends, rushes to get dressed, and runs off to the bar.

At times while he is hanging out with his friends, he recalls the videogame and feels a moderate yearning to play it. As he is returning home from the hangout, he looks forward to playing the game once more. He follows through with that intention, immediately taking up the game upon getting home, and again proceeds to play it well into the night.

Over the next several days the situation remains the same. Junseo cannot resist playing the game and is only torn from it when he must meet a few necessary obligations. At his leisure he does nothing else and ends up playing the game an average of 12 hours each day. During this time he constantly makes resolutions to stop, but then concludes to do so after 15 more minutes, after 20 more minutes, after another hour; he then defaults on his resolutions or loses track of time and ends up playing the game for multiple hours on end. When he does succeed in breaking free from it and leaves his room in order to eat or run some errand, as soon as he returns, he invariably resumes playing the game and continues to do so for hours and hours more.

This continues for six days. Then, at the end of the sixth day, Junseo finally succeeds in beating the game. And as soon as he does, he loses all interest in it and calmly stores his PlayStation away with no remorse whatsoever. From that point forward, he does not return to playing it or any other game and spends the rest of his winter break as he'd intended: doing his homework, hanging out with friends, and indulging his more mature and productive interests.

Certainly anybody who plays or has played videogames, or knows someone who does, will recognize that this isn't at all an uncommon occurrence. Of course it is just the other side of the procrastination coin, but this kind of behavior has some very intriguing peculiarities of its own. Videogames themselves are particularly interesting from a psychological standpoint. And we will later see the special kind of motivational conditions they create.

Oversleeping

Tom sleeps too much: 11 hours a day on average. Tom is unhappy with this state of affairs, but each day he is inadvertently coaxed by his circumstances to tack on those extra hours of sleep. He is in perfect health, physically and psychologically. And yet he has a hard time getting out of bed in the morning. Even when he wakes up fully rested, he often remains in bed and falls asleep for another hour or two or three. He has few obligations except for his job, where he is free to set his own schedule to conform to his day. He works from home on a computer in his relatively small one-room apartment, the same room in which he sleeps. After meals he often defaults to lying down on his bed, and this often turns into a brief nap. After finishing a part of his work, he also generally takes to his bed and once again inadvertently dozes off. He leaves his house to see friends, or go for a walk, or exercise at the gym almost every day, but aside from that he mostly remains in his small apartment. Other than lying in bed and sleeping, the rest of his day he spends working at his computer, pacing around his cramped room, and occasionally reading a book or watching TV, which he also does while lying in bed. Despite his exorbitant amount of daily sleep, Tom has plenty of time to meet all of his obligations, with hours left to spare for his waking leisure.

So, what of this example? Colloquially, this could be chalked up simply to laziness; otherwise depression, or perhaps some physical illness, may be suspect. And those can without a doubt be valid causes. Very often, however, even for such a straightforward behavior as sleep, the primary determining factor is motivation—and this is something that's usually completely overlooked.

I think these examples are sufficient in setting the scene and illuminating the problem that lies before us. We want to know: What are the elusive psychological mechanisms that underlie these behaviors so contradictory to our will? We want to know why we can't bring ourselves to do certain things and can't stop ourselves from doing others. Why is this kind of behavior so prevalent in human beings? And why is our willpower scarcely able to put up a contest against it? Why does doing certain tasks feel like lifting a giant boulder, while other activities are so alluring that we are unable to tear ourselves from them? And finally, we want to know why and how we are able to sometimes overcome this, what things we can learn from the times that we do, and how we can implement that knowledge to gain a greater control over our fates?

Chapter 2

Unraveling the Mystery

Without prematurely delving into any general psychological functions or theories thereof, we will be good to first sketch a few rough strokes toward a comprehensive picture which unites the examples in front of us. And here we can call upon a great insight, a notion that is well recognized today, in the difference between an act and its result.

The Act and the Result

It may seem at first glance that Jim wants to complete his paper, Annemarie wants to become fit, John wants to stop smoking, Junseo wants to quit his videogame, and Tom wants to sleep less. Their behaviors are thus incomprehensible to us. If we look closer, however, we will notice that what these people want are not those actions themselves, but merely their results. Jim doesn't actually want to write his paper, he wants the end result of writing his paper—namely, to pass his literature class. Annemarie doesn't want to actually *go* to the gym, at least not after the first two weeks, she also just wants its result—specifically, slimming down to her desired weight. John most certainly does not want to not smoke. Smoking brings him great satisfaction, he loves the taste of a cigarette and the calming sensation of the smoke—he only wants the final result: the health benefits, saving money, and being more pleasant to his friends and family. So does Junseo not want to quit the videogame; he is enjoying the hell out of it. He only wants the benefits of quitting: having free time to do other, more productive things. And finally Tom: He too only wants the practical benefits of not sleeping the extra three hours each day and having that time to do better things—but in the moment, the pull of slumber is too sweet for him to resist.

With just that distinction, then, it appears that the whole portrait has come together, and our initial puzzlement is entirely resolved. But not so fast! What we've reached is not the solution to the psychological mechanics underlying human action, but only the trailhead in our path to their understanding. After all, simply discriminating between an action and its consequences in no way tells us *which* factors determine whether a person will commit a particular action or not—or when he will commit it—or the ways he could be influenced to commit an action he otherwise wouldn't have (and vice-versa). For instance: Jim *did* write his paper; at least for two weeks Annemarie *did* diligently attend the gym; Junseo *did* quit playing his videogame; and John held out for a respectable while against his urges to smoke. Nevertheless, we have started on the right path, so let's follow it.

When the Result Outweighs the Act

If we look at Jim's behavior while separating the activity of writing his paper from its consequences, we can conclude that the reason he is able to finally write the paper is that the consequences of *not* doing so have become too dire. Once procrastinating any longer would have no other consequence than causing Jim to fail his class, rather than just causing him to write the paper later, the magnitude of the consequences begins to outweigh Jim's general distaste for writing, and causes him to overcome it.

We can therefore conclude that a person's desire for a behavior itself (for Jim, the actual process of writing his paper) and his desire for its result (in this case, passing the class) both contribute a motivating role toward whether or not he performs that behavior. Each exerts its own pull, and if the two oppose one another, the one that is stronger generally determines the person's manifest behavior. But what actually goes on in a person's mind that leads to him choosing one such action over its opposite?[2]

Anticipation of the Act and the Result

There are two different scenarios in the psychological battle between action and result that we need to distinguish. The first occurs when the person has not yet begun the action in question—for example, before Jim begins his paper. In that case, both the action and its result are merely prospective. They both exist in the mind as ideas, as anticipations of the future. The second scenario occurs when the person is already in the middle of the action, when he is currently engaged in it—for example, while Junseo is playing his videogame. In that case, there is a discrepancy between act and result, since the person experiences the act as something physical, present, and ongoing, while the result remains only a prospect, an expectation of the future.

In Jim's case, both the act of writing the paper and its result exist only in his mind, as prospects—neither are physically occurring to him at the present moment. And we know for a fact that the psychological factor that at last instigates Jim to write his paper is *anxiety*.

Thus, we can conclude that the emotion of anxiety acts as the future's ambassador to the present, for the consequences of Jim's actions—specifically, anxiety about what would happen if Jim fails to turn in his assignment. We can assume that a similar representative exists for the prospect of the act itself. And this we also know to be, in Jim's case, the overall *affect* of dread that accompanies the idea of writing his paper,

---

[2] After all, every behavior is only a symptom of the mental processes that cause it.

whenever Jim contemplates doing so.[3]

In light of this evidence, we can appreciate the large role that affect and emotion plays in motivating a person toward action. In any case, it is by no means a farfetched claim that future and/or prospective events bear on a person's present mind via the thoughts, associations, and affects they call up when thought about.

Present Activities versus Future Consequences

Now, in situations such as Junseo's, where future prospects conflict with a presently engaged-in activity (the videogame), we are able to gauge fairly well the kind of influences these two factors exert on a person's actions. For Junseo, who is so strongly bound by the activity of playing the game, it is clear that his future prospects have hardly any effect in compelling him to quit it. Since no considerations of the consequences of playing the game for so long (or about other more productive things he could be doing) are able to draw him away from the game for even an instant—despite such thoughts popping up quite often—we can conclude that, compared to his present experience of playing the game and the enjoyment he receives from it, those future prospects are not very potent. Some future events *do* make him quit his game, however; such as his plans to meet up with his friends. And these act upon him in the same way a deadline acts on the procrastinator: by prompting him to carry out his intentions at the very last minute. We also know that, in this case, that behavior is caused by precisely the same factor: anxiety—namely, his anxiety about the consequences of bailing out on his friends. Another

---

[3] To avoid future confusion on the part of the reader, I wish to underline the meaning of the word "affect." Affect, *noun* – A feeling or emotion. I will use this term throughout this book to refer to anything a person can feel, usually as a result of inner cognitive processes. Do not confuse it with the *verb* affect, meaning to have an influence on.

thing that makes him quit the videogame is a strong hunger.

What we see here is that this situation is almost identical to the one in which the action is only a future prospect. And that should not astound us so greatly when we realize that Junseo's case is merely the *negative* of the previous one. In Jim's case, Jim was trying to begin an activity (writing the paper). In Junseo's case, Junseo is trying to quit one (playing the videogame). But all it takes is rephrasing the state of affairs to see that the two are actually the same. We may say that Jim is trying to quit the activity of procrastinating (whatever *actual* activity that entails, and it may very well be a videogame). And we may say that Junseo is trying to begin a different activity (whatever he wishes to do instead of the game, such as meeting up with his friends). Each such scenario really has two parts: quitting one activity and starting another. It will be useful to keep this in mind.

Nevertheless, we can clearly distinguish a pattern here: It is the *concrete* future events, with concrete consequences, that most effectively motivate a person to act in opposition to his present desires. That for so many people, the motivating effect of an obligation takes place only at the last make-or-break moment, is due to the fact that *that* is when its impending consequences are truly *felt* (whereas at any earlier time, the perceived consequences are only of having to deal with the issue later).

That is not, however, because the emotion of anxiety begins to be felt at precisely that time. There is *always* an aspect of anxiety to this kind of impending obligation (although it is granted that at those last moments the anxiety is generally strongest). We must also not ignore that a strong feeling of hunger, quite similar in its psychological nature to a strong feeling of anxiety, causes Junseo to quit the game just like his promise to join his friends.

The Activation Energy for Starting an Activity

We've now accepted that much involuntary behavior, such as

the kind exhibited in our examples, is the result of a person having *opposing desires* for an action and its consequences: where either (1) the attraction of a particular activity overpowers the motivating power of its negative consequences, or (2) the motivating power of beneficial consequences is not enough to overpower the person's aversion to the activity that causes them. This, however, does not account for a lot of very similar behavior where these conditions aren't present; and it does not account *fully* for a lot of the behavior in which these conditions *are* present. That is because there remains one other factor we have not yet considered. Let us take, as an example, an extremely simple case in which a person has a definite (and non-ambivalent) *positive* desire for an action *and* for its consequences.

Chris wants to go play basketball at the court at his gym. He enjoys playing basketball, and it gives him a great workout in return. He has nothing better to do. But Chris lives 30 minutes away from the courts, and every time he considers going he thinks about the long walk it will take to get there, and then cannot bring himself to get off the couch. He ends up not going and watches TV instead.

In this scenario, Chris wants both the activity and its consequences; what he doesn't want is to take the actions needed to *commence* the activity. We may think that this is the hallmark of laziness, but what would we think if the walk was, instead, two hours—or four? In any case, every activity has this type of entrance barrier, a kind of activation energy. And very often it is precisely this entrance barrier that prevents a person from taking the actions he needs to begin an activity, even if that activity is both desirable in itself *and* beneficial in the long run.

In light of this, it seems that it would be best to consider the execution of an activity as consisting of two separate parts: the actions required to *begin* the activity, and the activity itself. Thus, in the mental contest between a prospective activity and its consequences, we must also factor in the actions that must be taken to begin that activity. Nearly always, those preparatory actions will act as a deterrent from engaging in the activity itself, since they are so often of a tedious, effortful nature.

If an activity is unsavory but its consequences desirable, this entrance barrier of beginning the activity serves as an additional opposing factor. If an activity is alluring but the consequences detrimental, the effort necessary to begin the activity can be the deciding deterrent that tips the balance toward abstaining. And if both the activity and the consequences are desirable, the preparatory action can *still* be enough of a demotivator to result in inaction.

In conclusion, after the resolution of the mental struggle between an activity and its consequences, the victor must do battle in yet another, similar struggle—between *it,* and the act of beginning that first activity. It is this second round of decision making that people so often butt up against, only to default to inaction right when they've gathered enough initiative to undertake an unpleasant activity.

And in the case of a person trying to quit in the middle of an activity he is already engaged in, the steps needed to do so serve the exact same role.

The Picture So Far

So far, we have made decent progress in roping in the issue of human motivation. Most importantly, we identified three psychologically separate parts to every activity—the activity itself, its consequences, and the effort needed to start it—which *may* conflict with one another in a person's mind, and pull him (by a psychological process we don't yet know) in opposite directions. I've represented this finding in *Figure 1* on the following page.

It seems, however, that we are now approaching somewhat of a dead end, and will soon be at a loss about how to proceed on our trail of inquiry. After all, analyzing behavior according to such general terms as *mental struggles, desirability*, and *deterrents* can only get us so far.

To gain any profound understanding of our current

problem, we must examine more microscopically the actual mental processes that occur in a person's mind when he is contemplating a future action and its consequences. Only then will we be able to determine the most significant factors by which he decides his course of action, and learn how to gain control over his actions by purposely manipulating those factors.

Indeed, it is very often the case in the scientific process that an intricate problem must be approached from multiple different angles before it yields a solution.

We will approach this problem, now, from the direction of introspective psychology; from which we can gain the most profound understanding of human motivation—and with it, the power to cure addiction, to increase productivity, to circumvent laziness, and so much more. And so, let us set off on this adjacent path that leads directly to a solution of motivation; and in the process, we will also attain the solution to our current inquiries at the point where these two paths intersect.

The Three Parts of an Activity

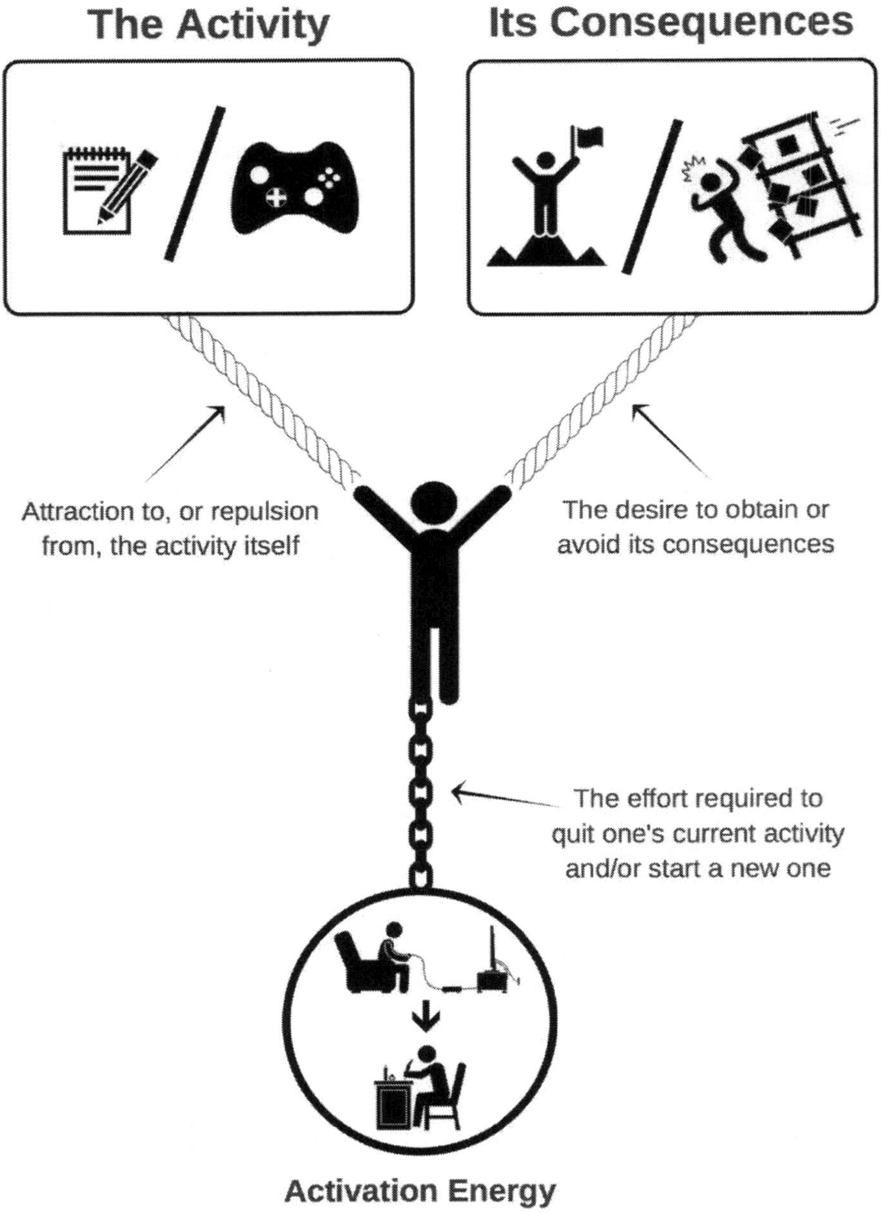

The Activity

Its Consequences

Attraction to, or repulsion from, the activity itself

The desire to obtain or avoid its consequences

The effort required to quit one's current activity and/or start a new one

Activation Energy

Figure 1

Chapter 3

The Psychological Nature of Motivation

We will begin by establishing the motivating (or demotivating) role of *physical* sensation. For the purpose of a rudimentary example, let us take two people with knee pain, with Person A experiencing more physical pain when walking than Person B. All other factors being equal, we can confidently predict that Person B will be able to walk farther than Person A before they both succumb to the pain and sit to rest. We can make the exact same prediction if we are dealing with only one person, Person C, at two different points in time: where at one time he feels more pain than at another, and all other factors remain equal. We can then say without a shadow of a doubt that he will stop sooner at the time when he experiences more pain. And the state of affairs cannot possibly be any other way. It is precisely in this manner that pain affects us. It motivates us to stop doing whatever causes the pain; and the greater the pain, the greater the motivation to stop doing it.

The true motivation a person has in this scenario and those like it is the simple one to get rid of pain, or at least to reduce it. And this doesn't only apply to physical pain. It is true of literally *everything* that has a pain-like, unpleasant quality to it. The greater the physical sensation of hunger in a person, the more he will be motivated to eat to relieve it. The colder a person feels, the more motivated he will be to find warmth. The greater the magnitude of an itch, the more compelled a person will be to scratch it.

It is also evident to us that when such a pain is being experienced it not only provides the motivation for the particular action that soothes it, but also takes motivation away from all other actions that do not—and this corresponds very strongly with its magnitude. Speaking of motivation in colloquial terms, a person who is extremely sick with a stomach virus, vomiting, fever, etc., will temporarily abandon all his aspirations and lose interest in all activities except those that provide some relief to his malaise. If he were to get a call from the president, he would likely tell him to call back tomorrow.

Now let us see if we can extend this principle to emotions. Nobody can deny the motivating power of emotions. Even in the most colloquial usages of the term, the role of emotions is implicitly acknowledged in this regard. Consider what answer an actor most often looks for when asking before a scene: "What is my motivation?" We have also seen from the examples at the start of this book how the emotion of anxiety motivates the procrastinator to finally write his paper and the video-gamer to finally tear himself from his game.

But there is no doubt that emotions such as sadness and anxiety and anger, whatever else they may do, evoke by their nature a physical displeasure. In addition, the actions any of these emotions motivate a person to undertake have the result of soothing or dissipating that unpleasant emotion (and sometimes also replacing it with a pleasant one). A person experiencing anger will seek to avenge himself on the person (or thing) he is angry at; when he does, the anger disappears. A person who is anxious will seek, usually, to avoid whatever evokes in him the feeling of anxiety; as soon as he does, his anxiety goes away. The function of sadness is more complicated, but it too generally makes a person withdraw from the saddening situation, and in this way at least soothes the emotion.

In light of this, we are obliged to conclude that the motivating role of these emotions is played in large part, if not entirely, by the *physical* feelings of displeasure that come alongside them. And by the most fundamental tenets of cause and effect, we can say with absolute certainty that: If the *only* effect those emotions had was eliciting the displeasure that is so characteristic of them, along with an inherent way of relieving it (such as revenge), they would produce precisely the same motivating effects on a person, at least in *quality*, as they already do. Really, what is the fundamental difference in the situation of an angry person who wants revenge (or an anxious person who seeks safety) from the hungry person who wants food, the tired person who wants rest, the nauseous person who wants to vomit, or the horny person who wants sex?

So too are there tons of examples in everyday life where these emotions compete with physical displeasure of a different sort—as equal opponents on a level playing field—to determine a person's actions. Consider that a shy child, who is too anxious to ask his teacher if he can use the bathroom, finally overcomes this anxiety when his need to urinate becomes too great. An adolescent who refuses to eat out of anger, in order to spite his mother, will find that his anger eventually succumbs to a more powerful feeling of hunger. And in nearly all cases, the deeply conscientious or religious person will come upon times when his natural sexual urges (which, by the way, definitely entail a feeling of displeasure and tension) will grow more intense than any feelings of shame he or she feels on the subject, and cause him to seek relief by way of intercourse or masturbation.[4]

From this exposition, we cannot help but get the impression that we've just unearthed a psychological mechanism of the most central importance for human functioning. It is the

---

[4] There are of course particularly rare and pathological cases in which the opposite occurs, and a person's emotions become so intense that they inhibit even the strongest physical motivations for the most rudimentary biological functions of life. And this always leads to, and exists alongside, a deep psychological pathology.

existence of a deep psychological need—or, more accurately, *compulsion*—to reduce displeasure/pain when it arises that motivates/compels humans to undertake the behavior required for carrying out all of their vital biological functions. What is even more striking is that this very same mechanism of compulsion is also responsible for a wide variety of much more complicated, and much less essential—even superficial—behaviors.

But before we address the generality of these findings, we must realize that we only have half of the picture. In addition to the need to reduce pain, we find that humans have an equivalent need to increase pleasure.

The Motivation of Seeking Pleasure

If we take a person in what we will call a neutral state, when he experiences no pleasure or displeasure, we will find the most clear-cut common characteristic in the endless variety of things he will seek. They will all be of a pleasurable nature. The person in this state can essentially be described as bored.[5]

In such a state, the person's mind will be drawn to and stay fixated on things that bring pleasure. And this does not only pertain to *actions* that bring pleasure. If pleasurable *activities* are out of his reach, the person will be compelled to seek that pleasure from *thought*. He will indulge in imaginative fantasies, recall pleasant memories, or contemplate something of interest. And if for some reason he is unable to do even that, and to attain his pleasure *consciously*, his unconscious mind will step in by way of associations and hallucinations, supplying that pleasure. It will strike up a song in his head, call up an encouraging chant or personal mantra, or place him inside a pleasant hallucination (as is so common in unconscious daydreams).

So, for whomever has wondered why during times of

---

[5] Boredom, of course, also has an unpleasurable quality to it.

idleness some song or tune would forcibly intrude into his mind—or why every so often he would inexplicably find himself mentally uttering a particular phrase or chant (always, by the way, of a self-extolling nature, or of a testament to having overpowered some hardship)—or why he is so often compelled to indulge in imaginative fantasy—or why his thoughts are so fervently and constantly drawn to a given activity (such as playing a videogame, or watching television, or pornography), on the basis of which we may conclude an addiction to that activity—the reason is that all those thoughts, ideas, and miscellaneous content that pop into one's head are of an entertaining, pleasurable nature. It is your mind sub-consciously trying to entertain you or lead you to pleasure.

But the mind does not simply want to obtain pleasure, it wants to *increase* pleasure. A person waking up in a neutral state will be quite content to take up a mildly pleasurable activity such as reading a book (one that isn't extraordinarily exciting, perhaps a textbook) or working on a creative assignment (provided that it does bring the person some pleasure). However, he will find it very difficult to do that same activity right after doing something that is *more* pleasurable (such as playing a game, or watching a TV show), since that would constitute an overall *decrease* in pleasure. He will experience the same dread and resistance against doing so that he would against a purely *unpleasurable* action (such as a chore that requires no urgency) when he is in a neutral state.

We can also observe this effect in the up-to-now puzzling, and rather disconcerting, mental phenomenon that most of us have no doubt experienced while reading a book. We notice that, at some point in our reading, we have in fact ceased to comprehend any of the content and have become completely engrossed in our own thoughts. We also know that once this has occurred, it becomes extremely difficult to resume reading, for little to no time will pass until that same thing occurs and we are again in our own thoughts. The reason for this is that the thoughts that usurp our mind bring more pleasure than does reading the book. And once the book has sparked interest in a more enticing and pleasurable train of thought, the activity of pursuing that thought is unconsciously adopted over the activity of reading. Otherwise, this same effect can occur if the book activates ideas of a worrying, or angering, or saddening nature, or if some other kind of displeasure comes upon us, which our thoughts then become naturally preoccupied with relieving.

In every instance that our attention strays so involuntarily and automatically from reading, it is invariably the result of one of these two factors: It is given up in favor of something more pleasurable, or because something displeasurable has been evoked. And this also holds true of all scenarios of a similar nature: of going off on a tangent in our own thinking, of our mind wandering when listening to a speech or lecture, and so forth.

The Ubiquity of Pleasure and Displeasure as Motivation

All the evidence we've just encountered testifies to the existence of a deep-seated psychological influence exerted by the *physical* sensations of pleasure and displeasure on many types of human cognition and behavior. We can describe the nature of this influence best as: a fundamental human compulsion to increase pleasure and reduce displeasure.

To psychologists in the late 19th and early 20th century, this was actually a widely recognized and accepted idea. Seeking pleasure and avoiding displeasure was then considered to be the most fundamental striving of the human mind, upon which all other psychological functions were based. Freud commonly referred to it as the *pleasure principle*. But this is no longer even a notion in modern Psychology today.[6] And yet we can con-

---

[6] After the so-called *Behaviorist Revolution* of the mid-1900s, all earlier psychological works, theories, and findings were labeled *unscien-*

clude, solely on the basis of our own evidence, that a very large portion of human motivation is undeniably determined by precisely this factor: the *pleasure principle*.

Certainly this realization alone is a huge gain (a reclamation really) in our understanding of human psychology and behavior. However, when we pursue this issue further, we come across an infinitely more astounding discovery. We find that there is *no* aspect of human functioning in which this element is absent, and that the pleasure principle, in fact, plays the lead role in directing the course of a person's behavior and thinking in every case.

If we become attuned to observing this effect in ourselves, we will notice that even the most trivial actions, such as getting out of bed in the morning, are wholly determined by this kind of pleasure/displeasure-based motivation. While lying in bed still provides pleasure (which it certainly does very often), a person will only be able to get up if some greater prospect of pleasure—such as excitement about starting a new day, or going for a morning run, or curiosity about the results of a sports game, or the desire to see a new episode of a beloved show—or else an immediate displeasure—such as an urge to urinate, hunger, the annoying sound of an alarm clock, pain from lying in bed for too long, anxiety about something that needs to be done, perhaps a stab of revulsion at sleeping too much—is experienced.[7] And even if lying in bed no longer brings pleasure, or even some displeasure (when one is no longer sleepy, and it becomes uncomfortable to remain in bed), the person will often require more motivation *still* to compel him to get up, since the actual act of getting out of bed is *itself* frequently

---

tific—and thus falsely contrived, nebulous, and irrelevant to today's science of psychology.

[7] This is true in most instances, for most people. But there are some other cognitive factors that a person can enact to help him with such behavior, as we will discuss later. (See *The Power of Imagination* section on page 82.)

displeasurable (especially if it requires exposing one's body to the cold, or takes a significant amount of effort, such as climbing off the top bunk).[8]

What our findings tell us is that the need to increase pleasure and relieve displeasure is not merely *a major type* of motivation, but the very essence of motivation itself. It is the active psychological force behind *all* motivation (much to the credit of 19th century psychologists), and anything that can be regarded as motivation derives its effect from precisely this source. And yet, despite its ubiquitous presence and its dominant, controlling role in all aspects of human cognition and behavior, unless this effect is made explicit to them, people are usually completely oblivious to the role pleasure and displeasure plays in motivating their lives. To them, it is entirely unconscious. While those who do notice their feelings tend to regard them as the result (or side-effect) of their thoughts and their actions, when in truth, they are the cause.

Recognizing now the pervading and orchestrating influence of this element, its most rudimentary binary functionality, and its uncannily unconscious nature, we can no longer have any doubts that what we are dealing with here is an entirely distinct unconscious mechanism in the human mind: the most archaic and the most important. Within the domain of our psychological theory, we must make a distinct place for it as a unique unconscious system in the human psyche.[9] Alongside the well-recognized and copiously studied *Associative Unconscious*, we can now add a second, entirely separate system that we will hazard to call: *"The Pleasure Unconscious."*

---

[8] In fact, we can regard any type of effort, no matter how slight or trivial, as evoking in anticipation of it some amount of displeasure: a displeasure that must be overcome by some source of motivation. And the greater the effort, the more motivation is needed to overcome the dread of that effort.

[9] One which is also, most likely, seated in a distinct area of the physical brain.

The Pleasure Unconscious in Animals

But once we admit this separate system as a key component of human functioning, we cannot ignore that most of the functions it controls, as well as its means to control them, are undeniably present in animals, too. In fact, the solely human ability of conscious volition, which is to a certain degree *independent* of the pleasure unconscious, while being our main counteracting force against it, is entirely absent in lower animals. So if the pleasure principle only roughly directs and controls *human* behavior, we can assume that it does so almost entirely for *animal* behavior. And this principle holds just as valid for organisms that reach all the way down to the earliest branches of evolution.

All this, of course, makes great sense. The pleasure unconscious recognizes only two inputs, pleasure and displeasure, and as its sole function propels the organism to seek the former and avoid the latter. This most basic binary functionality speaks of its ancient evolutionary origins.

Perhaps as early as some of the first origins of life, we could see this type of binary functionality in bacteria. Indeed, we still do today. A simple bacterium only needs to sense whether something is a necessary nutrient (good for it) and use its cilia to swim toward it, or whether it is toxic, harmful, and bad for it, and use its cilia to move away from it. If those weren't the actual evolutionary beginnings of the pleasure unconscious (indeed, it is hard to imagine that they were) its origin was at least rooted in the same reason. A rudimentary, simple organism would only need to avoid bad things and seek out nutrients. It is the necessary evolutionary start.

Once this first binary system is developed, the evolution of a more complicated organism would require more diversified functionality. Thus, with this binary groundwork already laid down, the natural course of evolution would be (and indeed seems to have been) to build upon it. At some point down the evolutionary line we can see the development of instincts and emotions, probably in that order, which appear to be built upon the pleasure principle in helping the organism adapt to its environment.[10]

We can then see, now for the much more complicated organism, that it needs not only to seek or avoid good and harmful things respectively, but that it also needs to perform a variety of other diverse tasks. Since introspection will tell us nothing about the instincts of animals, let us first talk about emotions and the functions they serve. It is clear that emotions are built upon the pleasure principle and that they motivate behavior in a particular way simply by the laws of the pleasure unconscious. The behavior that those emotions motivate is also, without a doubt, evolutionarily advantageous.

Take the emotion of anger: An angry person will seek to get revenge or commit violence upon whatever instigated that anger. Anger is itself unpleasant, and the ingrained biological way to get rid of that anger is by obtaining revenge—which also brings about a cathartic satisfaction, a great pleasure, when achieved. Anger is resistance to being harmed, retribution to the harmer. While it does not soothe the current injury it is a response to, it serves to protect oneself from future assaults by making it known to one's attacker that there will be consequences. We can clearly observe this in animals.

Or, take the emotion of anxiety: An anxious person will want to rid himself of the anxiety because it is displeasurable, and he will seek to do so by escaping whatever evokes that anxiety. If the anxiety is brought on by thoughts of a future action, he will seek to avoid that action. But if it is brought on by thoughts of *inaction*, it will provoke him instead into action. The evolutionary benefit of anxiety is, among other things, avoiding danger. And this we can certainly see in animals as well.

The whole range of emotions, the behaviors they motivate, and the benefits they provide, is too lengthy a topic to analyze here. But I will assert that *all* emotions operate on precisely that

---

[10] However, the line between instinct and emotion is blurred, and it is hard to tell whether they are not one and the same thing.

principle.

As for instincts, can we not surmise that an animal feels a great instigation, a nagging displeasure, to commit a particular act or movement when exposed to a stimulus? That a bird cannot help pecking when it sees red, because it causes it an unpleasant tension not to do so?[11] That a baby duck feels displeasure (anxiety?) when it is out of sight of its mother figure? That a fish has the compulsion to guard its eggs lest it feel huge discomfort or angst; and that it derives pleasure from doing so? That any animal when given the chance will know exactly how to mate because the motor notion of the act evokes inner excitement? Or that an animal voices a mating call to attract a mate, not as an unfeeling matter of course, but simply because that call feels satisfying—as a natural expression of its sexual yearning?

To follow the evolutionary steps of brain development further: We can infer that after the evolution of instincts and emotions (or perhaps at the same time) evolved associative memory, giving brains the ability to imprint and associate stimuli with the pleasure, pain, emotions, and instincts they once evoked. This development enabled creatures to adapt their behavior based on past experiences; it allowed them to learn.

That associative memory and the feelings by association it produces are, of course, still very strong in humans today. And it was only after all this in the history of evolution that the rational, explicit thinking and imagination unique to human beings finally developed.

---

[11] It is an instinctual behavior of a Herring Gull chick to peck at a red spot on its mother's beak, which prompts the mother to feed it by regurgitating food into its mouth. The chicks, however, will indiscriminately peck at a similar red spot wherever they see it, and no matter what it's attached to.

The Dynamics of the Pleasure Unconscious

Having listed all this, we can now appreciate the complex interactions of all that contributes to human behavior. The sensations from the external world, emotions, instincts, associative affect, and explicit imagination are all diverse sources of pleasure and displeasure that in some way affect human action and cognition. But in the end, all these act directly upon the first tier of motivation, and the highest court of appeal for all human physical and psychological assets: *The Pleasure Unconscious.*

It is based on this evidence that we come to our conclusion: that the major determining forces behind human thought and behavior are not *cognitive,* but *conative.*

We can thus gain a much more fundamental understanding of the influences behind human (as well as animal) behavior, if we think of every physical sensation and mental element—a thought, an idea, a memory, a belief—in terms of whether it is pleasurable or displeasurable, and every action and activity in terms of the way it increases pleasure or relieves displeasure.[12]

If we refer back to the procrastination example, we can see this principle in action most clearly. It may have puzzled us before that the emotion of anxiety, whose effect is notorious for producing avoidance, causes the procrastinator (in the final span of time before his assignment is due) to burst into a flurry of the most purposeful action. Not to mention that, until those final moments, the impending assignment *already* caused him a fair amount of anxiety, yet failed to produce an effect. The

---

[12] This is in contrast to the learning, reinforcement, and stimulus-response centered approach of the behaviorists. In fact, the very success that behaviorists attained, and the broad generality of their findings (of being able to categorize anything positive as reinforcement and anything negative as punishment), is due precisely to this fundamental two-way biological split between pleasure and displeasure, and the effects it has on the pleasure unconscious (something the behaviorists by no means explicitly recognize).

solution comes to us when we view his anxiety as *nothing other* than a displeasurable sensation the person experiences, when he contemplates the things that will happen if he doesn't complete his assignment. As long as there still remains time to dawdle, the unpleasant, anxiety-provoking thought of failing the assignment can be easily dismissed, along with its anxiety, by simply resolving to do the work later, and then brushing that thought from one's mind (and, truly, the thought and anxiety *both* go away right then and there). Once there's no longer time to waste, however, this maneuver ceases to work, and the only action that can relieve his anxiety (which is now at its strongest) becomes to physically *do* the assignment. [13]

Another extremely interesting fact to observe, is how intimately and inseparably a person's emotional responses to future events are tied to his actual expectations of them in reality: The procrastinator, for instance, no matter how hard he tries (and in the absence of mind-altering substances), will never be able to trick or convince himself that he has already done his assignment or that no real assignment existed in the first place. In the same way, a person who tries to impose a deadline on himself, knowing that there will be no manifest consequences, is utterly powerless to convince himself that there will be, or to conjure up any of the anxiety he so automatically feels when facing a real deadline with real consequences. Indeed, many of us meet with this problem in attempting to carry out our volitional undertakings, when we

---

[13] This same effect can be seen in a similar case of procrastination, such as the person who neglects to pay his credit card bill until the day it is due. That person will have an odd resistance to paying the bill beforehand, a greater resistance than is merited by any neutral action that calls for the same amount of effort. Because the very thought of not paying the bill brings anxiety, the person is actually compelled to avoid that thought because it is displeasurable, rather than relieving that displeasure by actually paying the bill (and this is of course easier than the physical task of paying it). The same thing also holds true for paying a parking ticket.

possess no external deadlines and have to answer only to ourselves.

Attention and the Pleasure Unconscious

There is one more issue I wish to discuss before ending this exposition. It has to do with multitasking: the fact that people have the ability to successfully engage in multiple activities at a time, as long as they are able to devote the necessary amount of attention to each one.

This is actually a psychological factor of crucial importance, but I will only briefly delve into it here. We know as fact that our capacity for attention is limited, finite. The actual amount we have at our disposal fluctuates over the course of each day, and some activities require a greater amount of attention than others.[14]

Our attention can be put to use for two functions: perception and action. The fact is that there is only a limited amount of information our senses can take in at once. We are able to perceive only a finite amount of the stimuli we are exposed to. In addition, it is not just stimuli from the external world that we can perceive, but our conscious thoughts and imagination, as well as our unconscious thoughts, associations, and hallucinations—all of these we experience through that same system of perception.[15] And all of these vie for the same finite amount of attention required to process them. We cannot listen to two speeches at once and understand both. If we read a book, we cannot also hold a conversation or think an independent thought. If we watch TV while playing chess, our analytical thinking in the game will suffer. In the same way, we cannot solve a very difficult math problem if we are also listening to music. We cannot think much when we are fully

---

[14] Tiredness or a large meal, for instance, significantly reduces our capacity for attention.

[15] We do actually hear and see them; and in the case of hallucinations, we are sometimes able to feel, taste, and smell them.

engrossed by taking in the external world, and vice versa. During dreams there is little to no possibility for conscious thought, and so is the hallucinating schizophrenic unable to really see the world or maintain control over his conscious thinking.

But voluntary action also vies for that same amount of attention. Just as feeling sensation in a body part requires attention, so too does moving that body part. In fact, the two are inseparable: whenever we lose sensation in a part of our body (by whatever means), we always find that we've lost the ability to move it as well.[16] Certainly, most of us who play a physical sport will have had an opportunity to observe that we will play worse and react slower whenever we are engaged in miscellaneous thought—when our attention is elsewhere. And when we take particular interest in observing something while walking, we often trip up.

We may regard observing the world and hallucinating to be passive perception. Conscious thinking, however, has a very definite volitional and deliberate element to it. And indeed, we do find that conscious thought and reasoning truly requires a huge amount of attention, even though the perceptual content it imposes on our senses (through the audible words and visible images it manipulates) is of no great magnitude.

The reason I needed to mention this topic of attention is that it is precisely *attention* that the pleasure unconscious exerts its control over in its aim to increase pleasure and decrease displeasure. It compulsively usurps our attention in service of thoughts, actions, associations, and hallucinations that work to bring us pleasure or relieve displeasure.

Lastly, we have to recognize that there always exists in us the

---

[16] Perhaps it will be discovered someday that voluntary movement and action differentiated at some point in evolutionary history out of perception, and that it's now merely a specialized form of perception as far as our nervous system is concerned.

strongest need to utilize *all* our attention. And this is quite evident in the great amount of displeasure we feel any time the entirety of our capacity for attention is not being put to use.

When this is the case, we will seek to find outlets for our unused attention. If we are playing a chess game with a weaker opponent, we will seek to supplement this activity with another: such as watching TV, or listening to music, or playing another simultaneous chess game. Very often this manifests itself in unconscious movements, such as fiddling around with something in one's hands or pacing around the room; and if such an action also serves to increase pleasure or relieve displeasure, all the better. [17]

Attention and Willpower

There is an interesting interaction here too, in that feelings of pleasure and displeasure simultaneously *direct* attention, and—since they are physical sensations—require attention to be perceived. And like with all stimuli, the more attention a person devotes to one, the more vividly he then perceives it. This, of course, is in full accordance with the functions of the pleasure unconscious, since the first thing a stimulus (whether painful or pleasurable) requires to affect a person's cognition, is to be perceived by him. It is thus only natural that the more intense a sensation, the more attention the person will automatically grant to it.

The curious nuance here lies in the undeniable fact that humans are able to exert some *conscious control* over where they direct their attention. We can recognize this ability, and the aptitude a person has for utilizing it, to be what people normally call *willpower*. This willpower is in fierce competition with, and is often overpowered by, the pleasure unconscious.

---

[17] Unconsciously breaking something or ripping it apart in one's hands helps frustration; making things neat and organized helps discomfort; and stroking one's own skin or hair soothes anxiety, reduces nervousness.

A person will indeed find it very difficult to devote his attention to thoughts or external happenings that bring him no pleasure and reduce no displeasure; and the times that he does, he will usually find that he's unable to maintain that attention for long.[18]

But a person's conscious ability to choose what he pays attention to, while mostly trumped by the pleasure unconscious when it comes to thoughts and external events, can also be used in another, indirect way to rein in his pleasure unconscious. The person can consciously focus his attention on the things he is feeling, and thus moderate (at least to some extent) the magnitude of their pleasure and displeasure.[19] This, in turn, allows a person who is experiencing multiple displeasurable affects to consciously select which displeasures he will deal with first—instead of being irresistibly drawn to the most intense ones—since he can, in effect, control their intensity.

Having taken this into account, let's now move on to the next chapter, in which we will further explore the nuances of willpower, attention, and the pleasure unconscious.

---

[18] There are times, however, (when the compulsions of his pleasure unconscious are temporarily satisfied) that he can do this; and these I will discuss later in the book.

[19] Generally, the more attention a person devotes to a sensation, the more intense it becomes: paying attention to an itch or a physical pain will make it feel greater, more intense, while taking his attention off of it will cause it to wane and (at least partially) subside. This phenomenon is responsible for many of the pain-moderating effects of hypnosis.

Chapter 4

How the Pleasure Unconscious Operates

We began this book with five examples of peculiar human behavior that occurred contrary to the better judgment and willpower of the persons committing it. Those and similar behaviors fall roughly into the categories of addiction, procrastination, and laziness: In each case the person was either very hard-pressed or unable to carry out the action he or she wanted, or had that same difficulty quitting an action he or she didn't want.

We then proceeded to evaluate the different opposing factors in a person's situation that would lead him to commit this behavior despite his better intentions. We found that it had to do with a psychological conflict between the actual behavior, the result of that behavior, and the actions necessary to begin or quit it. We ascertained that this kind of conflict could sometimes be influenced by the emotion of anxiety. But aside from that we were mostly at a loss as to what actual psychological forces were actively butting up against each other and opposing one another as the arbiters of this conflict.

We now know exactly what those psychological forces are at their most fundamental level: They are pleasure and displeasure. With this newly acquired insight we become able to both understand and correct the detrimental behaviors at the start of this book, and countless others like them. The key to this lies not in appealing to a person's logic or in cultivating his willpower, but in appealing to the deep-seated functions of his pleasure unconscious.[20] But before we tackle these issues head on, we will be good to take a more precise survey of how the pleasure unconscious operates, and take stock of the full arsenal of psychological weapons we have to redirect, control, and exploit it.

Displeasure Motivation versus Pleasure Motivation

There is a fundamental difference between the actions motivated by reducing displeasure and those motivated by increasing pleasure. For one, displeasure motivates a very specific course of action: the one needed to get rid of, or to at least partly soothe, that displeasure. Pleasure, on the other hand, can be attained from a variety of different sources.

A person will usually have only a few, if not just one particular thing that he can do to rid himself of his displeasure. Hunger can be best quelled by eating, coldness by warming up, tiredness by sleeping, stiffness by stretching, an itch by scratching, having to urinate by peeing, physical pain by removing whatever causes it, and so forth. And this holds true of emotions as well: The sad person will want happiness, an angry person will want revenge, the anxious person will want to escape the anxiety-provoking situation, and so forth. Assuming the necessary course of action is evident to the person, which it usually is, his attention will be powerfully drawn to thoughts of executing that action and how he should go about it. A hungry person will find himself thinking of food and how to get it; a tired person will think of snagging some sleep; a horny person will think about sex; an angry person will think about revenge, and so on.[21]

---

[20] We know that these first two methods just don't work, except when they also fulfill this last condition of tapping into the pleasure unconscious.

[21] There are, of course, times when a person will not know of any precise actions he can take that would eliminate his displeasure,

To increase pleasure is another matter. This compulsion is satisfied, at least to a quite large degree, by *any* increase in pleasure—whether it is a slight one from reading the news, a moderate one from listening to music, or a great one from having sex. A person in a neutral state of pleasure (bored) will have an affinity for all such actions if they're even a little pleasurable. What he actually ends up choosing greatly depends on other pleasure factors, such as how much effort (unpleasurable) it takes to begin it, and what consequences he can expect from it. It is in this scenario—where a person has a variety of possible actions before him, all of which constitute some gain in pleasure—that his willpower and rationale can have the greatest influence over his manifest actions.

The practical takeaway from this is that we should become aware of whether the behavior we are trying to control is motivated by relieving displeasure or acquiring pleasure—behaviors like smoking or masturbating can at different times and in the same person be motivated by either of the two or both. This is an important nuance to be mindful of, because dealing with each requires a different method.

Pleasure from Different Sources

A very important question to address is: How much control do we really have? Very often, if not almost always, most people feel that they have full control over their thoughts and actions; that they are masters of themselves and of their own fate. Is this an illusion?

---

especially if the source of that displeasure is complicated: A depressed person or one fraught with anxiety will frequently have no idea of the causes of his emotion. But even then, his attention will be drawn to this displeasure all the same, and he will most likely try to rationally figure out some course of action and/or solution for it. We can predict that his thoughts will then be generally consumed with grasping at solutions to his problem.

In large part: Yes. The pleasure unconscious is extremely obscure, and to notice it within oneself and make its existence explicit is horrendously difficult. It is so well hidden from our consciousness that we take for granted all its effects on us, its utter domination over our minds. It prompts no explanation and is in the most direct sense implicit.[22] And all the while, this utterly unconscious system is always seeking to be satisfied: it is always present, not simply in short bursts as our emotions are, but as a force that is in our lives *always*.

It is nonetheless true that humans are able to consciously exert some control over what we pay attention to. But this is in fierce competition with the pleasure unconscious. It will be very hard to focus on something that brings us no pleasure or reduces no displeasure. And most of those times that we do feel in control, we are simultaneously acquiescing to the strivings of the pleasure unconscious. If we try to fully recall a painful memory, or if we try reading a dull book that brings us no pleasure whatever, at every opportunity some association to something more pleasurable will pop into our minds, and if we try to dismiss it, we will not persist for long until something else that is pleasurable forcefully gains our audience.

It is, however, not an uncommon occurrence that we are able to devote our attention (or at least part of it) to something that only brings displeasure or is neutral. Our attention, after all, need not be devoted to only one thing: It can be split up—divided amongst multiple thoughts, activities, and perceptions. The pleasure unconscious, if no displeasure is currently being experienced, simply wants an increase in

---

[22] Just as a person often does not notice the role an emotion plays in directing his cognition—it comes upon him suddenly, and he has no mind to question why he wants to avoid something, or punch, or retreat into a hole, yet doubtlessly knows that he *does* want it, and can readily employ any rationalization to give a false reason for that want—it is even harder for him to recognize the much more basic, underlying part of him that's fundamentally responsible for *all* of those desires: the pleasure unconscious.

pleasure, and this can be satisfied with only a portion of our attention.

The pleasure unconscious isn't actually hard to satiate. Although the human mind will certainly seek pleasure when there is none, it is for the most part satisfied with just a small amount of it—or rather, a small increase in it. And a person is often able to meet this quota while only investing a small portion of his attention to do so. There is a great variety of ways to attain pleasure: Smelling a pleasant smell, looking at beautiful scenery or art, listening to music, feeling pleasure in a cool breeze or a hot shower, eating a tasty food, taking drugs, doing an intricate task, playing a game, exercising, reading an interesting book, experiencing a pleasant emotion, entertaining an intriguing thought, indulging in fantasy, listening to comedy, hanging out with friends, and so on and so forth. Some of these naturally require more attention than others, and some naturally provide more pleasure than others. And of course, there isn't a perfect overlap between the two.

It is when we are able to gain pleasure with only a part of our attention, that we are free to invest what remains into a thought process or task of our own choice. It is after all not unpleasurable to do chores while listening to music (or when drunk), to think about something neutral while biking or swimming, or to write an essay while drinking a sweet cup of coffee. And it is during the times when we waste little or no attention while experiencing pleasure, that we become capable of the greatest feats.

Pleasure is Relative

It is important to remember that the pleasure unconscious does not just seek pleasure, but seeks to *increase* pleasure. And this has very interesting effects on a person's manifest actions. If a person is experiencing a small amount of pleasure—for instance, if he is listening to a song that he likes while working on an otherwise unpleasurable homework assignment—he will not particularly seek to change his activity to something more pleasurable; even though he could easily devote the mental assets he's currently using to do his assignment to play a videogame instead, which he would certainly enjoy a lot more. Partially, this is because most of his attention is already invested in the double activity of listening to the song while doing his homework, and he has no attention to spare for thinking of more pleasurable activities. Another contributing factor is that the anticipation of a greater pleasure, such as he'd get from the videogame, is often not strong enough to overpower the *actual* pleasure he's already experiencing, and so does not much compel him to exchange that activity for another. A bird in the hand is worth more than two in the bush. But if that person's attention is diverted from the assignment for some reason (he gets a phone call) or the whole process becomes unpleasurable (he grows tired of the music or the assignment or both), he will be very compelled to switch to a more pleasurable activity, and will very often succumb to that compulsion.

A completely opposite effect comes into play, however, if a person attempts to switch from a very pleasurable activity (like a videogame) to a less pleasurable one (like listening to music while doing homework), even if it's still objectively enjoyable. This constitutes a decrease in pleasure, and the modus operandi of the pleasure unconscious makes the person extremely averse to such a change. He will have a very hard time relinquishing a large pleasure for a smaller one. And that transition is usually only achieved if something else displeasurable intervenes between those two activities.

It is because of this that we can speak of higher and lower pleasures. And it is why, to the person whose life is filled with the greatest ecstatic achievements and victories, the lower sources of enjoyment such as playing videogames, or getting drunk, or masturbating, are inherently unattractive as avenues of enjoyment.

The Pleasure in Activities

It should be well understood that when we regard an activity as *pleasurable*, it is only a summary of the whole range of nuances that occur during that activity. It is an average of the ups and downs—the pleasurable and unpleasurable experiences—that usually occur in rapid succession in most activities.

One factor that makes many activities pleasurable is that they consume a lot and sometimes all of a person's attention. And this, as we mentioned, is a very significant striving of the human mind—one that is also propelled by the pleasure unconscious. Playing a game (chess for example), or building a structure (let's say a table), or creating a painting, or writing a paper, or programming a website, or making a soup, and so on and so forth, all share the same characteristics of being very involved and often thought-provoking. We, of course, know that directed thought requires a huge amount of attention.

In each such activity, a person is constantly thinking of what the situation requires next; breaking the larger problem into simpler, smaller pieces; thinking over how he should go about accomplishing each piece; then physically executing the necessary actions; and finally moving on to the next hurdle. Although that process is not always pleasurable, each time he accomplishes a small step, if it was in any way difficult, he will naturally experience a tinge of the happiness emotion—he will feel satisfaction, a sense of accomplishment; and this is without a doubt pleasurable.[23] He will also feel a sense of anticipated relief and excitement from the prospect of reaching his goal, and bringing that activity to a successful end—this too is pleasurable, and it motivates him to continue.

An interesting nuance of this involvement in an activity is that the enjoyment a person derives from it greatly depends

---

[23] The emotion of happiness is automatically triggered whenever a person recognizes that achieving a pleasure or relieving a displeasure was the result of his own effort: that he was an active agent responsible for his own well-being.

upon his ability to engage in it. And this depends, in turn, on the amount of attention he's able to devote to the activity. It is for this reason that, when a person's capacity for attention naturally decreases throughout the day—when he becomes tired or eats too much—or if his attention is sapped by something else—he is distracted by something more pleasurable, or some displeasure forces him to devote his attention to it—the activity that had just before been pleasurable for him, now becomes distinctly unpleasurable.

This is partially due to him no longer being able to successfully execute the necessary steps in his task because he does not have enough attention to work through it—this deprives him of the *ups*: the bursts of happiness he feels when he succeeds in it. And partially, it is due to his new inability to consciously assess what steps to take next, or whether those steps are the correct ones—this leads to uncertainty and a feeling of dread, and even anxiety, about how the result of the task will turn out, as opposed to the anticipated relief and excitement he felt when confident of success.[24]

All the things that can be pleasurable about an activity are exhibited blatantly in games, and even more so in videogames. Each part of a videogame is new, filled with excitement and surprise (if the game is any good, that is), and the player must constantly achieve small goals and overcome hurdles in moving toward the final goal of winning the game. He is motivated by progressing in the game, which endows him with a sense of excitement and an anticipation of future fun, as well as a curiosity for what will happen next.[25] And because many

---

[24] And this usually causes the person to retract his attention even more from the task at hand, since it is no longer pleasurable: a positive feedback loop.

[25] Often a person playing a videogame will sympathize with the character in the game, feeling as if he himself is living in an exciting world of action and adventure, rather than just controlling a

videogames do not require very much conscious involvement in order to progress through them, they can continue to be enjoyable (even if somewhat less so) when the person is tired, or when his attention is split, or if it is in some other way diminished.

It is because of this perfect storm of pleasurable factors that videogames are so addictive. Interestingly, very much of their pleasurable effects are taken away once the person completes the game and already knows what to expect from it.

Pleasurable Emotions

Positive emotions are a very distinct source of pleasure. What makes them so unique and intriguing, from a motivational standpoint, is that they linger. That is, they can be a source of pleasure without taking up any attention at all. There aren't many positive emotions, as compared to negative ones: There is happiness, excitement, and affection/love.

Following a greatly triumphant event, the happiness emotion can remain as a lingering pleasure for hours, or even days, rendering a person free to devote the entirety of his attention to whatever he sees fit, without the oppressive imperatives of the pleasure unconscious bearing down on him, since they are already satisfied. In addition, these emotions are capable of providing a greater pleasure than can be attained from any other source. Indeed, these emotions provide the highest peaks that human beings are capable of experiencing.

Drugs may have a similar effect, but most drugs have a draining influence on attention and cognition in addition to providing free pleasure.

The Social Factor

As the astute reader may have noticed, I made little or no

---

character on a screen. And this is without a doubt very pleasurable, as well as addicting.

mention of interpersonal interaction anywhere in this book. In all five examples with which we started, the persons were isolated and stuck to try and deal with their problems all on their own. There is a very good reason for this.

The fact is, it is precisely those social factors—the influences other people have on our own experiences and motivations—that play by far the greatest role in obscuring from our consciousness the ever-present push and pull of the pleasure unconscious. That is because interpersonal relations are rife with emotions and other pleasures and displeasures, the influences of which most of us generally take for granted. There is almost always some kind of complex motivation in social conditions: We may try to make other people laugh, or they may do so to us; there are plenty of opportunities to be engrossed in conversation; we may feel anxiety about disappointing some people or being criticized by them; we may attempt to act on our sexual attraction to someone, or at least contemplate how to; we may find ourselves having to acquiesce to group activities we're lured to take part in, or have fun in group activities we truly enjoy. And in general, the process of social interaction contains many aspects of an involved and exciting activity.

Because most people are in these situations constantly and for the major part of their lives, they almost always observe themselves acting in rather reasonable, situation-directed ways. That is because the motivation from social situations is plentiful and powerful and intricate (humans are, after all, social animals), leaving people with little mind to consider the most fundamental psychological factors which underlie their behavior. And besides, human beings are quite poorly equipped to introspect in the first place.

It is when a person finds himself free from most or all social influences that he usually comes to discover in himself a great lack of motivation to do the things he had earlier considered important. Without anxiety about fulfilling what others require of him (such as at his job, or in school, or in a family environment), or excitement for gaining someone's praise (bragging about and showing off his accomplishments, or telling stories of his virtuous deeds), or the other great variety of pleasures and fulfillments that only interpersonal relations can provide, a person will likely find himself utterly dominated by the need to seek pleasure, and quickly default to the lowest and easiest pleasures available to him.

A person left in this way to his own devices, and at the unopposed mercy of his pleasure unconscious, will likely be consumed by it—at least for a while, until self-revulsion or some other factor eventually pulls him out of it. And many people who become mired in such a situation, as I have said happened to me, truly do eat themselves (I mean this *figuratively*, of course).

Chapter 5

The Mental Framework of Motivation

We have now, for the most part, become acquainted with the various nuances of the pleasure unconscious and the ways they manifest themselves in human behavior. In understanding how this system functions, we can now proceed to develop the methods to control it, and to use it to our conscious advantage. We will find it enormously helpful, however, to first examine the psychological framework inside the human mind where all these motivational conflicts actually take place.

The Three Parts of a Prospective Activity

It's finally time to pick up the reins of our first investigation, in which we divided a prospective task into three distinct parts: the actions necessary to begin it, the process of the task itself, and its consequences. These are undoubtedly real psychological stratifications that are an emergent product of the human mind, and not just useful categories that we picked arbitrarily to make our descriptive job easier. In a person's mind, each aspect is treated in its own specific way and usually affects him through a specific kind of pleasure or displeasure. I now want to make absolutely clear how this mental process occurs.

Each of the three parts of a future, prospective task contributes its own aspect of pleasure or displeasure when a person calls it to mind. This occurs because anticipated future—or simply imagined—actions and scenarios become somewhat real to a person when he thinks about them, which renders them capable of evoking pleasure and displeasure in the present.[26] Of course *all* feelings of pleasure and displeasure can *only* be experienced in the present, and that is precisely why thoughts of the future (like of the prospective tasks we are considering here) affect a person on par with the physical sensations he *presently* derives from external sources. In this way, the pleasure or displeasure a person feels when he thinks of a task compels him to either take it up or avoid it, all via the same fundamental unconscious process by which he (or an animal) would seek to move from cold shade into warm sunlight, but not when doing so would require stepping in filth or exposing oneself to danger.

The reason this usually serves us well, at least in satisfying the imperatives of the pleasure unconscious, is that the pleasure or displeasure we anticipate from a task (in each of its aspects) very strongly corresponds to the actual pleasure or displeasure we stand to experience when we engage in it. That is because our anticipations become unconsciously and firmly tied to our past experiences of a similar nature (when we engaged in that or a similar activity in the past). In other words, our anticipations are strongly tied to reality, or at least our experiential knowledge of it. In fact, it is unavoidable that this occurs. As we have already mentioned, it is virtually impossible for human beings to trick themselves into believing that the consequences of an action will be worse than they actually are (such as in self-imposed deadlines), and the same goes for the pleasure to be had in the act itself. We cannot help but represent the future realistically, at least to the best of our

---

[26] It is, indeed, a crucial function of the human imagination, that it allows a person to experience his thoughts and fantasies as though they were perceptions—as something akin to external reality, as something he feels to be physically happening to him.

knowledge.

There is no doubt that that kind of unconscious representation can be susceptible to flaws and inaccuracies: *It is*—and we will discuss some ways in which this happens. Nevertheless, the correlation between actual future experiences and our anticipatory mental representation of them is very high, and the more experience we have with a particular activity, the more realistically we unconsciously represent it as a prospect. It is a completely different story when we have very little or no experience with an activity (perhaps only book-knowledge). Then we are prone to represent it completely fictitiously, with very little correlation to reality, and often with a lot of anxiety besides.[27] And although the human mind *does* still attempt to unconsciously represent an activity the person had zero experience with, and knows little or nothing about, using as close an experiential analogue as it can find, this is usually so far off from an accurate representation of reality that it might as well be completely arbitrary.

Let us now look into the specific types of affect that each constituent of a prospective task generally evokes. Although it can certainly vary, the type of pleasure or displeasure a person experiences in relation to each of the three parts of a future task is most commonly the following for each one:

1.) *Starting the Task:* The pleasure factor of beginning a task most often comes from, and is generally proportional to (and hence a good representation of), the effort required to begin it.[28] As a result, it usually only evokes displeasure, since beginning any task requires some

---

[27] The emotion of anxiety is instinctually evoked when we are unable to *fully* imagine a future scenario or activity, while also expecting some danger from it.

[28] This is assuming the person knows what he must do to begin the task. But if the task is a new one, he is likely to overestimate or underestimate what it will take, based on whatever information he has to go on.

amount of effort, which is pretty much *universally* dis-pleasurable.

2.) *The Task Itself:* The pleasure factor of the task itself usually derives from the actual experience the person anticipates from the task, usually based on his experiences with it in the past.[29] It also greatly depends on the pleasure or displeasure the person is *currently* experiencing (we will recall that pleasure is relative).[30] Generally, this amounts to a good representation of the pleasure the person will *actually* derive from the activity when he engages in it.

This representation can, however, be somewhat inaccurate because of a subconscious tendency people have to favor recent experiences over more distant ones, and displeasurable experiences over pleasurable ones. It is most inaccurate when the person has no first-hand experience with the activity at all, and bases his anticipation of it on whatever meager information he does (or doesn't) have. In those cases, it may be supplemented with the displeasure of anxiety.

3.) *The Consequences:* The pleasure factor of the result of the task is usually emotional. The anticipation of the result

---

[29] I should note that this is not the same as a *summarized average* of the ups and downs of the task, as I mentioned in "The Pleasure in Activities" section. There I was referring to an averaging of the experiences during the course of the activity—when the person is in the middle of doing it. With that, we could make general statements and say that the activity is, as a whole, pleasurable or displeasurable. In this case, when the task is only a future prospect, a person will actually have a manifest *pleasure-representation* of the task in his mind; and it will be an anticipation of that task as a present feeling of pleasure (excitement) or displeasure (dread).

[30] Sometimes the idea of peeing will be highly pleasurable (that is, when the person is overwhelmed by a great discomfort from the need to urinate). And sometimes the idea of playing a videogame may be distinctly displeasurable (usually, when the person is already engaged in something more enjoyable and fulfilling).

most frequently evokes either the emotion of excitement, or the emotion of anxiety. But it can also evoke disgust, or an anticipation of relief, or a feeling of dread.

Those three dimensions of a prospective task, along with their commonly evoked affects, are illustrated in *Figure 2* below.

The Main Pleasure and Displeasure Factors:

(All Contribute Toward Whether the Person Takes Up the Activity)

How Difficult it is to Begin:
(Dread of Effort Proportional to Its Difficulty)

Starting the Activity

+

How Pleasurable or Unpleasurable it is (or appears to be):
(Anxiety may also be present)

The Activity Itself

+

The Reward When the Task is Completed and/or the Detriments if it isn't Completed:
(Usually Emotional: Anxiety or Dread vs. Excitement)

Its Consequences

and / or

Figure 2 —

It is important to note that in *Figure 2* we are, so to say, attempting to represent a three-dimensional structure in just two dimensions. These three aspects of a task are actually involved in a very *real* thought process—mostly unconscious—that occurs in a person's mind when he considers whether or not to take action. And during this person's actual thought process, all these aspects of a task *do not* come to his mind all at once. Rather, they appear in succession, even if sometimes a very quick one, occurring within a timeframe of just a few seconds.

Almost always, the first thing that comes to a person's mind is either the notion of the task itself, or the idea of its consequences: thoughts of what he must do to start the task naturally emerge later. Furthermore, a person does not *always* consider all three parts of a task before reaching a decision. Sometimes, he will just consider the idea of the activity itself (if it is a particularly enjoyable one) or its consequences (usually when they are especially pressing), and that alone will be enough to compel him to undertake it. It also isn't uncommon that a person will engage in a task without paying heed to its consequences *at all*, even if he fully knows what they are: They simply may not come to his mind at the time, or he may deliberately avoid thinking about them.

An overwhelming majority of the time, however, all three constituents of a task *do* come to the person's mind, and each plays its part in moving him to engage in the task or refrain from it. This is especially so when a person is on the fence for whether to take up a task or not. Then, these three aspects may come to his mind *perpetually*, and he will become occupied with the painful deliberation of weighing the three aspects against one another. For instance: The person may think of an errand he has to run, then imagine how unpleasurable it will be to actually do so, and when deciding that the juice is still worth the squeeze, finally think of the effort he must exert to begin it, and end up doing nothing at all. He may often remember this errand (namely the consequences of leaving it undone), and again and again go through the same thought process, and obtain the same result, perpetually wallowing in inaction. Other times, the person may consider a pleasurable action, then think of its negative consequences and/or the steps he must take to begin it, and be discouraged from it in the same way, to once again end up doing nothing. This too is likely to be a perpetually occurring chain of thoughts, and also lead—in most cases—to inaction.

Motivation for Continuing the Current Activity vs. Beginning a New One

In *Figure 2* we have depicted the pleasure-incentive of a prospective activity, and we can use that as a model for making rough estimates of how alluring the idea of that new task will be. But if we want to be able to predict whether a person will actually take up that activity or not, we have to include in our model two other factors.[31] This stems from the nuance we mentioned in Chapter 2: that starting one activity also means quitting another.

We can view anything a person is currently doing as an activity, even if he's just lying on a couch bored out of his brains. This is useful because it lets us gauge how much of his total attention the person is currently employing, as well as how much pleasure he is currently experiencing. With that we can compare the pleasure and displeasure he derives from his present "activity" with the gain in pleasure he stands to experience from a prospective one. And more importantly, it lets us ascertain the *consequences* of *quitting* his current activity, which certainly play a key motivating role in whether the person does or does not quit it.

We know for a fact that the procrastinator rushing to write

---

[31] Doing all this, of course, requires knowing the amount of pleasure and displeasure each part of the task will evoke. And although determining this may not be an easy or precise job when dealing with others, it is a fairly tenable one when dealing with our own feelings and behavior.

his term paper at the last minute is prevented from switching to a more enjoyable activity by the consequences of doing so: failing his class. In that case, anxiety plays the role of an overseer: administering a sharp jolt of painful affect (as if slapping his hand away) whenever the person considers quitting and switching to another task. Thus, anxiety doesn't just make the person finally begin his assignment, but also prevents him from quitting in the middle of doing it.

We can, of course, view the consequences of quitting the current activity as just a part of the consequences of beginning a new one, but there *does* exist a psychological distinction between the two within a person's actual thought processes. Although sometimes the two sets of consequences come to a person's mind simultaneously, often a person *does* think of them separately, and regards them subconsciously as two separate entities. It may just be a matter of semantics, but our depiction in *Figure 3* below should represent the matter fairly.

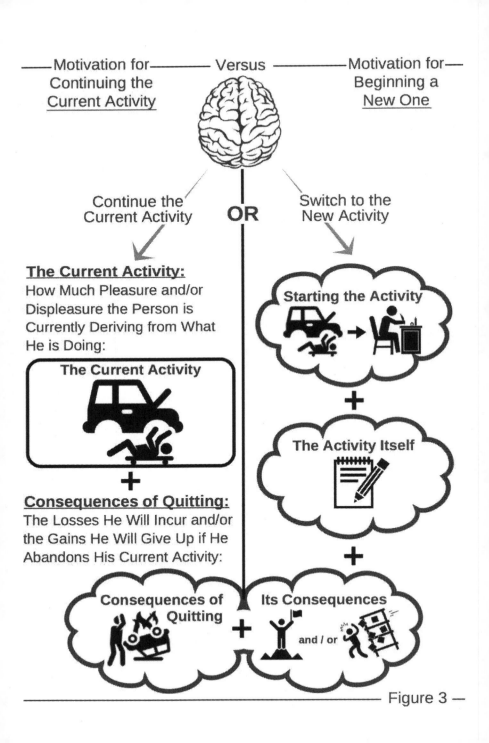

Figure 3

As we have shown in *Figure 3*, a person's manifest behavior—of whether he switches from one activity to another—depends on the combined pleasure incentive from the three aspects of the prospective task, as weighed against the amount of pleasure he derives from his current activity, plus the pleasure-based consequences of quitting it.

This will be a good model to refer to in the next chapter, in which we will survey and dissect the various psychological tools we can use to influence the pleasure unconscious, and thus indirectly control our behavior.

The Role of Willpower

But looking now at this model, we cannot avoid addressing a very important question that's really at the heart of this book: What is the role of willpower? The understanding of motivational forces that we've reached and diagramed in *Figure 3* seems to leave no place for willpower in a person's decision-making process. Surely a human being isn't just an automaton who invariably follows the path of least resistance toward pleasure and lacks any volition of his own. What of the people we encounter who are incontrovertibly strong-willed, consistently able to postpone or forgo pleasure and remain tough in the face of displeasurable adversity? What of the abstinent? The austere? The morally pious, who resolutely follow what they think is right, and appear to largely disregard their personal discomforts and pleasure-lust?

It does indeed seem that such people have a force of will much greater than the average man, making them able to successfully oppose and override the pleasure unconscious. That is, however, almost certainly not the case. While humans do have the ability to consciously direct their attention independently of the pleasure unconscious (that is what we recognize as willpower), and by the principle of human variability, we can assume that some persons have a much greater aptitude for this than do others, there is no evidence to suspect that this alone constitutes that seeming ability of some people to live outside the laws of the pleasure principle.[32] Instead, every bit of evidence suggests that these people's ability to constantly overcome the pleasure unconscious by sheer force of will is merely an illusion. They most likely differ, primarily, not in their ability to behave contrary to motivation, but in the types of motivation they experience and the magnitude of the affect they feel in response to certain situations.

We know for a fact that those people who most commonly exhibit a willful restraint of their pleasure unconscious-based impulses, the religiously pious, actually do so (at least in the vast majority of cases) out of anxiety. They have a unique anxiety-provoking factor that is absent in non-religious persons: a fear of God. We've already learned that a person feels anxiety in response to consequences he thinks to be real, while being utterly unable to conjure up anxiety for consequences he knows will not happen. A religious person who

---

[32] On the principle of human variability: Nearly every measured aspect of human biology and psychology has been found to vary throughout the population and be distributed on the normal distribution curve. This has been recognized as an emergent property of the fact that nearly all human traits—biological, psychological, and behavioral—are highly multidetermined: meaning, they are each the result of many different influences acting in concert. Given the large number of factors contributing to a trait, it's very unlikely for a person to end up possessing *only* those that affect it positively (or negatively); and much more likely for him to possess some combination of both beneficial and detrimental ones—hence, the normal distribution curve. In statistics, this has been called the Central Limit Theorem, which states that when taking a large random sample of different variables (even when those variables are nowhere near normally distributed), their averages *will* be normally distributed, as long as those variables are largely independent of one another. This can be confidently assumed of most human traits—and without having to posit anything as to the nature of their contributing factors (whether those are genetic, learned, or otherwise).

believes—or is at least wary of the possibility—that God exists, physically experiences anxiety about committing actions, and even having thoughts, that are not in accordance with the moral precepts of his religion. He really does feel himself being watched and judged by God, liable to incur eternal damnation in hell for his actions. He fears this just as he would fear a physical axe over his head. And just as anxiety for not meeting a deadline motivates a person to act in order to avoid the consequences, so does anxiety motivate the religious person to act as he was taught is *right*, lest he incur punishment from God. By no means does this person live outside the laws of the pleasure unconscious, and it is most clearly by those very laws that he *only appears* to overcome it by the force of his will.

A similar factor is also responsible for the seemingly will-powered constitutions of many non-religious persons. Even with no fears of otherworldly punishment, people may possess unusually strong sources of motivation in their lives (usually of a social nature) that most others do not.[33] Also very importantly, however, people can differ not just in the types of motivation present in their lives, but in the magnitude with which they feel the affects (usually emotional) that motivate them.

Many of the *strong-willed* persons so remarkable for acting on their convictions and not on the dumb impulses of the pleasure unconscious may do so not because they *will* them-

---

[33] These may be positive (pleasure-seeking) as well as negative (displeasure-avoiding). A person may be exceptionally motivated by a desire to gain the praise and approval of a parent, or to prove his worth in front of a potential lover, or to be accepted into a community, or to accomplish something he values higher than anything else. Oppositely, a person may desperately fear chastisement from a parent, or a friend, or a teacher, or a lover, or being excluded from a group or community, or failing to achieve his most important goals. All these, of course, often can be—and are—true of religious persons as well.

selves to, but because they feel a particularly intense affect in relation to the consequences of their actions. The conflict between our convictions and the pleasure unconscious is, after all, essentially a conflict between the pleasure incentive of the action itself and of its consequences.[34] We can assume by the same principle of human variability, that some people experience a more potent emotion than others—some may feel a fiercer anger, a heavier sadness, a brighter happiness, a more cutting anxiety, and so on. This may simply be a part of their inborn, genetically determined temperament.

Can we not then suppose that the person we consider *strong-willed*, who undertakes a displeasurable task in order to reap its beneficial consequences, does this because the idea of its results brings him more pleasure, more excitement than those identical consequences would for the average person? Or when the strong-willed person forgoes a pleasurable activity with negative consequences, may it not be because he naturally feels a greater anxiety or a more poignant shame and self-revulsion (this is an emotion I will discuss shortly) in anticipation of those consequences than the average person does? Or maybe such a person inherently experiences less pleasure during the pleasurable activities, and less displeasure from the displeasurable ones. In any case, all these are possibilities and may very well coexist in a single human being, since they don't contradict one another. Perhaps it is the person in whom all or many of these factors are present that we are prone to consider exceptionally strong-willed, as opposed to a person who only exhibits a strong will in certain isolated areas of his life.

Surely all this accounts much better for the disposition of people who appear to defy the imperatives of the pleasure unconscious through sheer volition. There is, however, no reason to assume that a greater capacity to consciously direct one's attention does not *also* contribute some modest part to

---

[34] The person acting on his convictions is doing what he considers best for himself (or for those around him) in the long run.

this type of strong-willed constitution. It likely does. But it is almost certainly not capable of being its sole determinant, and thus going against the most fundamental and archaic psychological functionality of the pleasure unconscious.

As for how willpower *does* affect a person's decision making, we've already mentioned the conditions under which it has freedom of reign and is mostly unrestricted by the pleasure unconscious:

1.) When there are multiple available activities, all of which constitute an increase in pleasure. The person can then relatively freely choose between them.

2.) When the compulsion to increase pleasure has been satisfied already, with only a small portion of the person's attention. He can then invest his remaining attention as he wishes.

3.) When the person is experiencing displeasure from multiple sources: He is then able to decide which to deal with first.

All this, of course, is entirely consistent with our model in *Figure 3*. And being thus reassured of the validity of our model, we can proceed to using it as a reference point in the next chapter, where we will examine the various techniques at our disposal for influencing the pleasure unconscious to achieve our chosen goals. So, without further delay, let us do just that.

Chapter 6

The Strategies in Our Toolbox

Our aim in this chapter is to list the various methods we can use for combatting the maladaptive behaviors instigated by the pleasure unconscious. We will also note which aspect of a current or prospective activity each method affects, and how it does so.

The Displeasure of a Guilty Conscience

The first psychological weapon a person has against the detrimental behaviors spurred by his pleasure unconscious is the powerful sense of remorse and self-criticism he experiences when he commits an action he disapproves of—when he goes against his conscience. This is a distinctly unpleasurable feeling produced by the emotion of shame and/or guilt. In most cases, a person instinctually experiences a guilty or shameful remorse during or sometime after committing an action different from what he believes to be the correct one.[35] The same negative feeling can also be experienced in anticipation, when a person only entertains the idea of committing an action that he morally disapproves of.

---

[35] For more information on this emotion, see my book *Depression and the Immature Romance: The Secret Inner Battle of the Depressed Mind.*

This undoubtedly belongs to the psychological domain of an action's *consequences*. It can be felt while a person is in the middle of a regrettable action (such as playing a videogame, or masturbating, or not going to the gym). It then serves as a motivator for quitting that activity and taking up something better. It can also be felt in relation to a prospective activity. Just as a person can feel an anticipatory excitement or relief when he imagines completing a beneficial task, so can he feel an anticipatory shame or guilt when he imagines engaging in a task he considers lowly or ignoble. This anticipated negative affect then acts as a deterrent against beginning that task.

In fact, the emotion of shame and/or guilt is essentially our unconscious mind's pleasure-based envoy of our conscious intentions—it is what allows those intentions to affect our manifest actions by influencing the pleasure unconscious. After all, it is precisely with the *consequences* of our actions that our deliberate intentions and goals are concerned.

One serious problem is that although the emotions of guilt and shame do serve as demotivators against committing the actions a person wants not to, they all too often aren't potent enough to prevent him from committing them. We've all certainly heard of guilty pleasures.

In the five examples with which we began this book, every one of those persons would have felt these negative emotions. Yet that clearly wasn't enough to stop their detrimental behaviors; and in most other similar situations, it *alone* isn't enough either. Much of the time, this emotional response merely backfires. It fails to have any physical effect on a person's negative actions, but is felt as a residual effect of committing them—which only serves to reduce the person's confidence and self-esteem.

Nevertheless, it is still a very useful source of motivation—or rather demotivation—toward choosing the activities we know to be good for us and avoiding those that we know aren't. And since motivation stacks up (it is, after all, merely a quantitative battle of pleasure versus displeasure), it is a step in the right direction, and can be supplemented with other sources of motivation that support the same ends.

Keeping the End in Mind

It is important to mention, that because what we consciously desire always coincides with the consequences of our actions, it is a big help to actually *remember* what those consequences are, and to keep them in mind when considering a prospective action. We already noted that this doesn't always occur, and is not entirely automatic. So it is a very good idea to make a habit of purposefully recalling the consequences of the actions we are compelled to take up.

Do not Weigh Pros and Cons

Perhaps one of the greatest anomalies of our rational mind is how it tends to completely acquiesce to the imperatives of the pleasure unconscious. If we attempt to approach a problem armed only with the faculty of reason, without making use of any fixed beliefs or negative associations, our rationale will likely lead, often very irrationally, to precisely the conclusions that bring us the most pleasure or reduce the most displeasure. This is the well-known process of rationalization, and there is perhaps no time its effects are more blatantly evident than when we attempt to *reason out* whether a particular course of action is the correct one.

We naturally do this by weighing the pros and cons of an action against one another, and forming our conclusion based on that balance. (This, of course, pertains exclusively to the *consequences* of that action.) What happens most of the time, however, is that our deliberations uncannily conform to the compulsions of the pleasure principle; leading us to conclude that activities which are pleasurable are also beneficial, and the activities which are unpleasurable are not—often when this is objectively untrue.

What occurs psychologically during this weighing of pros

and cons is that the pros of a pleasurable action seem at the time to fully justify it, even if they are objectively fickle or worthless; while the cons seem to be utterly insignificant, even if they are objectively great. Once again, we are brought to appreciate the utterly non-obvious fact that our mind holds pleasure and displeasure as the main currency of our psychological transactions.

For example: To a tired person lying comfortably in his bed, and weighing the pros and cons of getting up and starting on a productive day, against remaining in bed and snagging some extra sleep, whatever fickle pros of returning to sleep he thinks of—the vague health benefits of resting more, that he can get the same things done even if he wakes up four hours later, that he might be too tired to get anything accomplished, that the morning chatter of birds may be too distracting for him to get down to work, and so on—will carry great weight because they are imbued with the immediately felt (and quite substantial) pleasure of the comfortable sleep he is drawn to, while the pros of getting up—the knowledge that waking up early always brings him great satisfaction, that he usually works best at this early hour, that he has already slept more than enough and will only get more tired from the extra sleep, and that the things he can do if he wakes up are the best use of his time, while sleeping is objectively worthless—will affect him only very little or not at all, because he doesn't truly *feel* the pleasure that comes with them.

Compulsive sexual actions are a particularly common victim of this. As a very insightful friend of mine once said (in relation to the prospect of having sex with an ex-girlfriend): "Whether it is objectively for the best or not, I can't trust that at the time I won't be able to convince myself that it would be." In these kinds of situations, when we are drawn to an action we know to be wrong and that we'll regret later, the key isn't attempting to reevaluate whether it's actually so (even if we are strongly impelled to). For if we do, we'll almost invariably find ourselves overwriting our previous convictions, and taking up the unintended action as a result. In such situations, it's best to form our conclusions beforehand, and then stick to them (remembering that they are more valid than whatever our reasoning will generate in the heat of the moment).

The Power of Habit and Association

To not go through the fallacious process of weighing pros and cons while still making use of the influence of knowing the consequences of our actions, it is best to make a strong associative connection between the thought of an action and the thought of its consequences. Strong associations like this usually take a while to form and require a substantial amount of repetition to do so. The process is basically one of forming a habit of thought: to deliberately call to mind one thought in relation to another (in this case, thoughts of the consequences in relation to thoughts of the action). After doing so many times, the process will become largely automatic. The result is a quick association of a displeasurable thought (usually an off-putting picture or vision imbued with a negative emotion) to the pleasurable thought of a detrimental action. Or, it can be the association of a pleasurable thought to that of an unpleasurable action. This serves as a kind of immediate pleasure-based counterweight to compelling behaviors we know to be detrimental.

The reason I recommend this kind of association and habit-forming is that it is quick and mostly unconscious. Being unconscious, it isn't subject to much conscious scrutiny and reevaluation via the pros and cons process that we know to be so harmful. But its biggest advantage is without a doubt its quickness as an automatic reaction, since there are many situations where time is a large factor in our decisions of whether to engage in an action or not. Sometimes we will find ourselves in the middle of an activity before we have any time to think of its imminent consequences, and automatic association often works to prevent such behavior. There are, however, times when even a habitual association is too slow to prevent this: like in our example with the smoker at the start of this book.

Controlling our Environment

It may seem an outdated behaviorist notion, but the most powerful and effective way to change our behavior is to change our environment. This is undoubtedly true. However, unlike behaviorists, we are wise to admit that this is an *indirect* method of influencing our actions: The state of our surroundings has a definite bearing on our thoughts, which only then contribute to our behavior. Nevertheless, it is much more effective than trying to control our thoughts directly and deliberately.

This is nothing new. We had already, in effect, reached this essential conclusion in admitting the following two notions:

1.) The distribution of our attention, and thus the contents of our mind, are much more strongly determined by the pleasure unconscious than by any of our deliberate efforts or intentions.

2.) The pleasure-seeking thoughts that *do* compulsively occupy our mind cannot help but be strongly rooted in reality.[36]

It follows from this that manipulating our external environment will have profound effects on what activities compel us and what our manifest actions will then be. And this proves very true in practice.

By purposefully manipulating the surroundings in which he lives, a person can alter the motivation he derives from any aspect of nearly any activity. He can intentionally change his surroundings to make the effort needed to begin a particular

---

[36] This second notion refers to the fact that for all three aspects of an activity—the effort needed to begin it, the process of the activity itself, and its consequences—our anticipatory awareness of them, and the affect it carries with it, corresponds precisely to what we expect them in reality to be; and we are utterly unable to deceive ourselves as to the truth of that reality.

task physically greater.[37] He can introduce certain factors to make the process of the activity itself a less pleasurable one.[38] And he can create various self-imposed consequences to an activity to make its results undesirable.[39] Of course, if he wishes to increase his engagement in an activity, he can do the exact opposite, and make it easier to begin, more pleasurable to take part in, and have beneficial consequences.

Targeting the process of beginning a task is particularly effective. Physically changing our surroundings to make that process easier or harder can make all the difference in our manifest actions: It can induce us to take up beneficial activities that we otherwise wouldn't have, and entice us to refrain from detrimental ones that we'd otherwise take up. The very notion of doing so, however, is usually overlooked by most people; especially in the case of detrimental activities.

Let us take for example the videogame addict who cannot help but play a particular game whenever he has a moment to himself. With what we now know, we can say with great certainty that a big factor in his behavior is the easy availability of the game—he needs to exert virtually no effort to begin playing it, except perhaps turning on his computer (if even that).

What would happen, then, if he takes preventative measures and stores his videogame cartridge in a safe-box two miles away from his home? He would certainly still pine for the game since the thought of playing it brings him pleasure. But then he'll have no choice but to imagine the long walk to the

---

[37] We've already seen a good example of this in the smoker who makes it physically harder for himself to retrieve a cigarette, thus deterring himself from the act of smoking.

[38] For example: A person who wishes to quit the habit of biting his nails can coat them in a bitter-tasting nail polish, thus rendering the act itself displeasurable and unsavory.

[39] For example: A person who wishes to refrain from getting drunk can authorize a friend to take $20 from him if he does.

safe-box and back, which he needs to take in order to play it, and most likely not go. Sometimes he'll get dressed and ready to go to the safe-box, but then he'll remember that he is trying to quit the game, and that that would be pathetic, and not go. Sometimes he'll make it halfway to the safe-box but then turn around and go back. Sometimes he'll make it there and hold the game in his hands, but then decide against it. And sometimes he will actually succumb, make the entire journey there and back, and end up playing the game despite everything. But in total, he will play the game incredibly less often than he would if it was already in his computer. And eventually, since he is deprived of it, the impulse will slowly fade.

As we can see from this example, the time aspect also plays a large preventative role in these kinds of scenarios. If manipulating one's environment has the additional effect of not only making the start of an activity require more effort, but also more time, the person will have more opportunities to think over (and consider the consequences of) whether he really wants to go through with it or not—and thus have more chances to bow out. Indeed there are many activities, especially those that only require a click or two on the computer, that require so little time and effort to start that the person doesn't have even a moment to think of the consequences (or of anything really) before he finds himself right in the middle of one.

Of course the same principle works in the other direction as well. A person can preemptively reduce the time and effort needed to start an activity, and thus be more enticed to actually take it up.[40] Somebody who has to spend a lot of time traveling to somewhere he wants to go will invariably be deterred from it for that reason. If a person must, every time, clean a bunch of clutter off of his desk and struggle to plug his lamp into a hard-to-reach socket so he can make space to read a book

---

[40] Time is of course inseparable from effort. The amount of time required to do something corresponds very strongly to the amount of effort required to do it.

(even one that he's excited to read), he will invariably be deterred from doing so. If he *preemptively* cleans his desk and gets an extension cord for his lamp, however, he will no longer be inhibited by this in his ambitions to read, and be much more compelled to actually do it.[41]

The main trick to making these kinds of prophylactic changes to our environment is first realizing where such changes need to be made, and then deliberately making them at a time *estranged from* the activity that calls for them. The video-gamer will find it very hard, if not impossible, to store away his videogame at the moment when he cannot even resist playing it. And the person who wants to read a book but is unable to even overcome the effort needed to clear his desk in order to do so, will certainly not go further *still* and put in an *even larger* effort setting up his environment so he can make his future reading attempts easier.

This is really the main reason why people go without making such useful changes for so long and so often fail to do so entirely: It is that they are only confronted with the idea of making such a change when they are defeated by the situation that calls for it—in other words, at the precise time when they want the exact opposite. Once the person has already refrained from the compulsion of an activity that required too much effort to start, or succumbed to an activity that was instead too easy to start, he loses the immediate need to change those conditions and most often puts the notion of it out of his mind until he is once again confronted with the activity that calls for

---

[41] For activities that require a long travel time or commute, it is admittedly difficult to reduce that time without making drastic changes to where one lives or acquiring new modes of transportation. A good way to tackle this, however, is to take the opportunity to travel someplace at precisely the times when one is already near it for other, more important reasons. In that vein, one can make plans to travel to a certain place to take part in multiple activities available there, and thus make use of multiple sources of motivation to overcome just one required amount of activation energy.

it. The result is that people perpetually butt up against the same motivational problems of starting an activity and never do anything to change them.

The solution, of course, is to realize that those changes do need to be made and that they would be decidedly beneficial; then, keeping that in mind, deliberately making those changes at a miscellaneous time when one has enough motivation to do so. It is when the video-gamer is morally repulsed with playing the game, or tired of it (for the meantime), that he should take the opportunity to lock it away, instead of—as most people do—simply forming a resolution to not play it later: a resolution that is almost invariably broken. Similarly, it is when the reader is feeling industrious, cheery, that he would be best to go out of his way and improve the reading conditions on his desk, treating this as a necessary chore.

It is important to reiterate that most people only experience such a total paralysis before taking proactive actions to change their surroundings if they were never able to overcome those surroundings in the first place. It is the reader who can never overcome the activation energy of clearing his table in order to read, who is most likely to never make any preemptive changes to make it easier. And it is the video-gamer who can never resist playing his game anytime he's compelled to, who is most likely to *not* lock it away. On the contrary, however, the reader who *does* frequently (or at least occasionally) overcome the needed effort of clearing his table, and the video-gamer who fervently tries and sometimes succeeds in resisting his impulses to play the game, are actually very likely to take the necessary prophylactic measures and to change their environments to accommodate their goals.

To those who have to *physically* experience displeasure in the effort of starting or refraining from a task, because they have to go through that same displeasurable process every time they do so, it is actually quite natural and automatic for them to seek and take measures to make their experience more agreeable. The reader who constantly finds himself spending time and effort clearing his desk before reading, will naturally find a way to make this process permanently easier. The video-gamer who, in being drawn to his game, perpetually and painfully fights his own impulses in order to avoid playing it, will likely support those efforts by physically doing something to help himself in that battle, and soon lock away or otherwise dispose of the game.

It is in cases where people *do not* actually go through the displeasurable effort of starting or refraining from a task, and are instead defeated by it, that they are prone *not to* facilitate their struggles by improving their surroundings, and to not even realize that doing so would make a difference. But unfortunately, such cases are plenty.

A second, similar method of changing one's environment to change one's motivation is targeting the pleasure (or displeasure) derived from the task itself.

The activity of hiking may be inherently enjoyable to a person, but it will be much less so (if not entirely a pain) when he is doing so in ill-fitting shoes that create and continuously aggravate painful blisters on his feet. If he has only those shoes available, he will be greatly discouraged from going hiking altogether because he will anticipate it as an uncomfortable and painful process. Getting comfortable shoes, of course, immediately fixes this problem both practically and motivationally. And people are actually very keen on making these kinds of physical changes in their lives—ones that make desired or required activities easier or more pleasurable. [42]

It is making these kinds of helpful changes, but in the negative direction, that most people have a very hard time wrapping their minds around. For example, to purposely leave oneself with only uncomfortable shoes if one's goal is to *not* go hiking. Or, more practically, to deliberately buy only bland,

---

[42] In fact, most technological progress in the history of man has been devoted to precisely this goal: More comfortable shoes, more efficient plows, faster transportation, sharper knives, and so on and so forth, from the history of prehistoric tool-making to that of industrial machinery and modern electronics.

tasteless food if one's goal is to eat less; or to intentionally make the conditions in one's home uncomfortable and unaccommodating if one's goal is to spend more time outdoors.

That very notion of purposefully making life harder for oneself is met with substantial resistance by most people, and is in general completely counterintuitive. The average person will consider the idea of doing so absurd, and resolve to battle with his unhealthy compulsions through his personal will-power, without resorting to such ridiculous measures. Of course we know that these efforts through *willpower* are extremely fickle and almost invariably doomed to fail, especially when the person butts up against the same motivational conditions every time. On the other hand, there is no doubt that our alternative method of physically changing the environment is directly effective and reliably yields great practical results.

Lastly, a similar change in motivation can be effected by targeting the physical consequences of various actions. This method is not at all an automatic modus operandi for most people. In general, people accept and deal with the set consequences of their actions prescribed by their surroundings. It is, however, possible for a person to personally manipulate and create consequences for his actions; and this will inevitably have an effect on his future motivation and behavior.

Most often this is achieved through the imposition of monetary consequences. A wager is a quintessential example of this. A person striving to reach a difficult goal or complete a task—building a porch or losing weight, for instance—will be wise to supplement his motivation to do so by making a bet on it with a friend. He would of course bet in favor of himself; and in doing so, he will receive both a positive incentive to complete the task (his desire to collect the reward for winning the bet) and a negative disincentive to quit the task (his desire to avoid having to pay out if he loses). Of course the more money he bets, the more motivation he will receive—assuming he finds someone willing to bet against him. On the other hand, the repercussion-free bets that are commonly deemed "*friendly bets*" will have little to no motivational impact because they impose no consequences.[43]

Of course consequences, and even bets, are not restricted to monetary ones. One interesting kind of consequence a person can impose on himself is an automatic exposure to embarrassment. If he wishes to not take part in an activity he is ashamed of, and would be embarrassed if he did and his friends found out, he could set up conditions that would make it impossible for him to hide his behavior from those friends. Today there are many online applications that can be used to accomplish this: Ones that automatically post your activity on social media or allow people access to your browser history, and so forth. Such tactics really do work, since a person will anticipate the unavoidable embarrassment that would result from his actions and be more motivated to refrain from them instead.

It does indeed seem that nearly all self-imposed consequences to one's actions require the involvement of other people to be enacted. All wagers undoubtedly require someone to wager with. The same is true for all situations in which a person relinquishes a certain power over himself to another, to be exercised if he engages in or fails to perform certain actions.[44] So too for situations in which one person is voluntarily sponsored by another, who then rewards him for performing virtuous deeds and refraining from detrimental ones. Those are, after all, essentially one-sided wagers, where the person exposes himself to either just risk without reward or

---

[43] It seems that a real friend is someone who is willing to stake money to bet *against* you, and the more the better—but only if that bet is made with you, of course.

[44] For example: Giving a friend the authority to take your money, or to do something else that would be decidedly unpleasant for you.

just reward without risk.[45] And that covers just about the whole spectrum of self-imposable consequences, pretty much excluding only those analogous to an automated electronic device that hits you with an electric shock every time you pick your nose, or some kind of demented mechanical contraption that lowers a boulder hanging above your car a few centimeters every time you masturbate.

I want to make one final point about changing the physical environment around you to curb the unwanted yet compulsive behaviors instigated by the pleasure unconscious. It is that the tides of the mind are turbulent. A person's mind is subject to undergo drastic changes in mood, cognizance, pleasure-lust, and other factors affecting his motivational state even over the course of one day. There will be times when he experiences compulsions that are too strong to resist, and times when his power to consciously resist them is too weak. There are indeed moments of great temptation and moments of utter weakness before it; there are moments of complete irrationality, and moments when rationality is impotent; there are great tide-changing bursts of emotion, and times of insufferable boredom; and they all occur sporadically and inevitably in the microcosm of one human mind.

Any changes we try to make in our thinking, in an effort to curb our unhealthy compulsions, will therefore be vulnerable to a variety of insubordinate forces from within—which will usurp or override our conscious cognition and volition, and cede control of our actions to the more basic, archaic systems in our mind. We should now be aware, after all, that we have astoundingly less control over our own minds than we initially thought, and the times when we are in control are only those in which the pleasure unconscious allows us to be. We also know the kind of ill mental health and neurosis that can arise in the

---

[45] In terms of motivation, however, it is clear that a conventional wager is a much better choice, since it provides incentive at both ends: with both risk and reward directed toward the same action.

person who attempts to guard against his subconscious compulsions at all costs, by means of only his conscious faculties.[46] This person is implicitly aware of the erratic nature of his mind, viscerally experiencing as he does the moments when his forbidden impulses are chomping at the bit to be acted on, and when his mind is ready to betray him—this kind of man truly *doesn't trust* his own mind.[47] He will indeed have to be constantly on guard against those times as well, and usually this results in a huge restriction of his activities (usually via anxiety), since he must defend against situations in which he may succumb to his own impulses. Resulting symptoms are likely to be something along the lines of agoraphobia, paranoia, and obsessive compulsive disorder.[48]

But while changes in one's mental state are sporadic and our control of them tenuous, the physical environment around us is practically static and our control over it is only restricted by our physical limitations. We can make resolutions to behave a certain way and it is uncertain whether we'll even remember them, let alone be able to act on them, when the time comes. But once we change something in our surroundings, it is bound to stay that way (barring some rare external forces). A person who's made a resolution to read the next time he wants to watch TV, may—even when he is utterly bored—have the very notion that there's an opportunity to do so entirely slip his mind, or be unable to act on it even if he does remember.[49] On the other hand, what *will* help him keep his resolution when he wishes to watch TV, is butting up against the cold, hard reality

---

[46] The person who, for example, is morally repulsed from any sexual urges, or the person who is constantly on guard to not accidently reveal some shameful secret about himself—which is also, very often, of a sexual nature.

[47] And in part, we know he is right to.

[48] Of course, most compulsions that give rise to disturbances of this magnitude are not likely to be preventable by means of a simple change in that person's environment.

[49] This sort of thing is a very common occurrence.

that his TV isn't there because he stored it in his closet and replaced it with a book two days earlier. Many unhealthy compulsions are in this way capable of being nullified: when the opportunity to act on them is made physically unavailable.[50]

Employing Social Motivation

You can make good use of the motivation derived from other people in helping the vicissitudes of your pleasure unconscious conform to your conscious goals.

1.) Doing things with a friend can make otherwise dull activities exciting and fun instead. This can be implemented to make starting activities easier or less unpleasurable: What would otherwise be a long, boring commute can be an enjoyable time if you make it with friends.

2.) It can make activities themselves more pleasurable: Working out or putting together a presentation can be made much more enjoyable with a social aspect added to it.

3.) Social aspects can also contribute to the consequences of certain actions: Promising a friend that you will do something will make you anxious about failing to fol-

---

[50] The pleasurable emotions our imagination evokes cannot help but be intimately linked to reality, and our mind does not derive much pleasure from impossibilities. Most of the pleasurable ideas that compulsively occupy our mind are those that have a chance of becoming reality. A person addicted to a videogame will only feverishly think of the game when there is a physical possibility of playing it. Once there is no such possibility, he will no longer derive anticipatory pleasure from such reveries and they will cease to so compulsively intrude upon his mind. Thought presupposes action: If there is no possibility for action, the thought quickly loses its appeal too. And just as a person is unable to call up any anxiety for a consequence that he knows won't actually happen, so is he unable to conjure up much excitement for the prospect of playing a game he knows is unavailable.

low through, and thus much more likely to actually do it. The incentive to appear virtuous in front of friends can motivate you to actually behave more virtuously in turn. Rivalries and competitions are often a great source of motivation for bettering yourself, working at something, and doing the best you can to excel at it. There is, without a doubt, an abundance of possibilities to use the social motivation we naturally derive from other people to reach our deliberate goals.

Splitting your Attention

We've already mentioned that we can subdue the wants of the pleasure unconscious by using tactics of divide and conquer. The compulsion to increase pleasure can be satisfied and put at bay with only a small portion of our attention, leaving the rest of it free at our disposal. We can then devote that attention to productive, if tedious, tasks like cleaning, cooking, exercising, and so on, without the normal aversion to their unpleasurable nature, since we are already receiving pleasure from elsewhere. This method pertains, of course, to the process of the activity itself.

Splitting our attention between (1) mundane and not very involved tasks and (2) some enjoyable but similarly uninvolving activity, not only makes those former tasks effectively pleasurable (or *more* pleasurable), but also allows us to mobilize the whole of our available attention—another big striving of our unconscious mind. Effective sources of pleasure that don't consume much attention include listening to music, playing some mechanical game, chewing gum, or eating a tasty food or beverage. People commonly partake in these in conjunction with necessary and largely unpleasurable daily activities in order to make them more bearable.

This is a great method for activities that don't require much attention to perform; however, it is inherently unsuitable for mentally involving activities that necessitate one's full attention to carry out—these include reading, writing, mathematics, and so forth—since it is likely to distract from those activities instead.[51] But it is important to watch out, even during just partially engrossing tasks, that the pleasant activities you supplement them with don't take up too much of your total attention, and render you unable to devote the amount required to the actually important, primary activity. For example: A person who multitasks by playing solitaire and listening to a speech may find that while he was initially managing the two tasks well together, the solitaire is beginning to take up too much attention (this can happen for a variety of reasons) and he is missing a lot of the speech. Or the person who listens to music while writing, may find that his mind starts to stray too often from the writing, and becomes more and more consumed by the music.

Directing your Attention

I wish to touch here upon a point I made at the end of *Chapter 3*.

We know that humans have the conscious ability to direct their attention, but most times it is overpowered by the attention-drawing power of the pleasure unconscious—mostly ceding attention to prospects of pleasure and manifest affects of displeasure. However, because perceiving pleasure and displeasure also requires attention, we can actually direct our attention *consciously* in order to manipulate the magnitude of our affects and thus the pleasure unconscious. We can exploit this ability in situations when we are simultaneously experi-

---

[51] Although in those cases, there are still peripheral activities that can provide a source of pleasure with virtually no required attention. Aesthetic pleasure from nature fits that bill: looking at nature's beauty, smelling a fragrant odor, feeling a pleasurable sensation on the skin from a cool breeze or a warm sun, and so on. It's no surprise, then, that people are more motivated when working outside on a beautiful day, and that insightful thoughts come more freely and abundantly in a beautiful, natural setting.

encing multiple sources of pleasure and/or displeasure, and use it to propel actions that are in closer accordance with our conscious goals.

It is possible to deliberately sink our attention into a particular source of pleasure or displeasure and thus make it more intense. And if that attention is transferred from other sensations of pleasure or displeasure, it will also serve to make those sensations *less* intense. Just as a mild itch gets significantly more uncomfortable when we think precisely about it, and we then become extremely compelled to scratch it despite consciously knowing that it would only do us harm; so can we consciously direct our attention toward a small pleasure or displeasure, and use it to overcome a much greater and fiercer affect.

For example: A person who consciously wants to get out of bed, but is paralyzed by the pure physical pleasure of remaining in it, can leverage a slight displeasure to propel him to get up. If he feels a slight amount of discomfort or strain in his rib (tiny in magnitude compared to the pleasure of lying in bed), he can direct his attention only at that tiny displeasure, and use it as a fulcrum by which to extract himself from his nest.[52] This method pertains, of course, to the pleasure or displeasure derived from a present activity.

Employing Emotion

Emotions are great sources of motivation and usually yield powerful amounts of pleasure or displeasure. And we can harness the abundant motivating power of emotions by consciously redirecting it toward productive behaviors. Emotions are by their nature malleable, and while they instinctually motivate towards a specific *type* of action (like

---

[52] By a similar effect, when a mother strokes the hair of her sick child, it soothes him by allowing him to redirect his attention from his pain and/or nausea to the pleasurable feeling of his mother's caress.

causing some harm to the person anger is directed at), the actual actions that we choose can be to a large extent determined by our conscious mind.

For example: A person angry at his wife for slighting him can seek his revenge by insulting her, destroying or defacing her possessions, or possibly even causing her physical harm.[53] He can also suppress his anger and incur a substantial amount of stress. These are clearly bad alternatives. He can, however, consciously channel his anger into a productive task like setting up his fishing gear, finally replacing the tire on his bike, or some other manual task required for a hobby of his, through which he can temporarily *get away* from his spouse. This will still get revenge on her (in a way), and so at least partially satisfy his anger; and in return, the anger will serve as motivation to do what would otherwise be a boring and unpleasurable task.

This method of rechanneling emotions is applicable to positive emotions in addition to negative ones, but with a key difference. Negative emotions, like anger or shame, can be redirected toward productive ends, but only if those ends also satisfy the emotion's natural, instinctive compulsions (like getting revenge or making amends). Positive emotions like happiness and excitement, however, are not restricted to being redirected towards a particular purpose, since they are for the most part ends in themselves—they are *free pleasure*. Happiness *does* subconsciously draw a person to dwell and reminisce upon its source, and excitement subconsciously pulls the person to plan and contemplate the idea that excites him, but at the same time both are residual sources of free pleasure, and the person can take up any other task instead, and find it fairly pleasurable because he is already experiencing pleasure from those emotional, chemical sources.

In the case of negative emotions, this method of redi-

---

[53] Usually, that is the natural, unconscious path to action towards which anger motivates. It subconsciously drives a person to take revenge on the person who incurred his anger on an *"eye for an eye"* basis.

recting an emotion pertains to the consequences of an action, since it is the result of the action (the man getting away from his wife) where the satisfaction lies. In the case of positive emotions, however, it pertains to the process of the action itself, since that action now becomes—and is anticipated to be—more pleasurable, due to the free pleasure derived from those emotions.

The Power of Imagination

The next method is an extremely crucial one, and has a particular psychological importance. It pertains to the start of an activity. When starting an activity requires only physical movement—such as getting off the couch, or putting on clothes, or entering the water at the beach—the simple technique of imagining yourself physically performing those movements has the uncanny effect of compelling you to actually execute them. We know that even the simplest actions necessary to start a task—like getting up off the couch, and moving oneself to a writing desk—can be incredibly hard to overcome for the person who lacks sufficient motivation to do the actual task they start. And even when his motivation *is* sufficient, or when it is a close call between beginning that new action or not, the activation energy of those simple physical movements—especially if they are displeasurable, like getting up off a comfortable couch—will often be enough to inhibit that person from taking any action at all. But this activation energy can be easily overcome, without incurring any displeasure, through the power of imagination.

The trick is to deliberately and in detail imagine yourself, best in first person, performing the physical movements you need to make. This includes imagining how you will move your arms, your legs, your body, and so forth. It generally takes a second or two to imagine this, and after you do, you'll soon find yourself—perhaps to your own surprise—automatically springing into action, and performing those movements without giving it any further thought, and exerting practically no effort (this usually occurs upon taking your mind off the subject). Give this a try; it is a truly odd trick, and works as a shortcut to overcoming the activation energy of many activities.

I see two reasons why this works. The first is that after imagining yourself performing physical movements, your body experiences a sort of uncomfortable tension if it doesn't actually execute them. By way of the pleasure principle, you then seek to perform those movements to relieve that tension. The second reason is that imagining actions, particularly movements, before performing them is the standard modus operandi of the connection between your body and mind. Consider the times when, in walking somewhere, you automatically make it all the way there along a certain path without giving it any thought whatsoever: This is invariably because on the start of your journey, you imagined (for a brief second, sometimes entirely subconsciously) the path to that exact location. This is most noticeable when you accidently end up at the wrong place: when you decide in the middle of your journey to go elsewhere but fail to trace that route out in your mind and end up at the initial destination, only to then realize that you no longer have a reason to be there. Also consider the times you automatically, without giving it any thought, perform all the actions necessary to go to the bathroom or retrieve food from the fridge, and only become cognizant of the fact that you did so when you are in the middle of peeing or eating. It is because you invariably traced the route and actions out in your mind before doing so. The same phenomenon occurs when you contemplate saying something during a conversation, maybe an offensive comment, and finally conclude to withhold saying it, only to suddenly find yourself blurting it out anyway during some opportune moment.

Caffeine and other Drugs

We've already mentioned the free pleasure that can be attained through chemical means, using various drugs and substances.

Many drugs have the effect of free pleasure, which is what makes them so attractive in the first place—with the additional effect that they also restrict attention and/or cognition. Alcohol, for example, is one such drug. If you are set on a task that requires a high level of cognitive work and available attention, it is not a good idea to drink alcohol for motivational purposes. It is *okay*, however, for rudimentary tasks like chores around the house.

There are, however, some drugs that provide free pleasure without having any detrimental effects on cognition. Caffeine and tobacco are popular examples of this, and they are very effective substances.[54] We can think of the effect of caffeine or tobacco as being the chemical equivalent of listening to music without devoting any attention to doing so. In undertaking a large, effortful, and generally unpleasant task, it is often extremely helpful to do so with the help of caffeine and even tobacco. These two also have the added benefit of bringing physical pleasure in the action of ingesting them. Drinking coffee, for instance, brings pleasure because it tastes good, and smoking a cigarette or chewing chewing tobacco brings pleasure because the act of doing so is physically satisfying.

Making use of drugs in this way pertains, clearly, to the activity itself: making a current activity more pleasurable and a prospective one *appear* more pleasurable.[55]

---

[54] Tobacco, we know, is highly damaging to long term health; while caffeine appears to be pretty much harmless in this regard.

[55] One negative side-effect that caffeine has, but tobacco doesn't, is the all but inevitable "crash" that comes a few hours after ingesting it. In that respect, it *does* have a draining influence upon cognition, but that effect is a delayed one. Caffeine can therefore be viewed as providing free pleasure *now*, in exchange for diminishing cognition in the near future. But, if managed properly, its benefits for motivation will—in most cases—far outweigh its drawbacks.

Frustrate a Need

Another interesting motivational technique is frustrating a present need or desire and using it instead as a reward for a less desirable action. Hunger, a want of leisure, the desire for a cigarette, sexual impulses, and the like, can yearn for satisfaction and distract you from your present task. This call to satisfaction, however, can be repurposed to be not a deterrent, but an incentive. The trick is to reframe it in your mind not as an alternative to your current activity, but as a reward you will procure after completing it. This is achieved by setting a concrete goal to reach in whatever task you are currently working on—writing a certain number of pages, or cleaning a certain part of the house, or finishing a particular assignment, and so forth—and resolving to reward yourself with the satisfaction of the desire you're belaying after you meet this goal. Setting up your environment to facilitate this type of future reward over immediate satisfaction is also very helpful to this end.[56]

This method is pretty effective but should be used sparingly, since it generally causes a person to incur a fair deal of stress. Also, belaying things like hunger can cause detrimental biological effects as well. The aspects of a task it pertains to are the current activity, from which it removes negative affects (at least partially), and the consequences of the activity, to which it adds the incentive of satisfying a desire. The effect is turning a displeasurable distraction from a current activity into additional motivation for completing it.

Monitor your Attention Capacity

It is very important that, in your attempts to intelligently modulate the motivation for achieving your goals, you be aware not only of your current states of motivation but also of

---

[56] For example: Having your place of work be separate from the place where you eat or smoke.

your capacity for attention. Your total attention capacity varies quite significantly over the course of a day, being influenced by factors including tiredness, digestion, and blood sugar. Some activities require a truly large amount of attention: for example, solving difficult physics problems, reading dense literature, or programming a complex application.

If you simply do not have enough attention at your disposal to devote to a task, no amount of motivation can help you. Plus, the activity is bound to quickly become displeasurable because you are unable to successfully perform it. It also helps to be aware of your attention capacity in cases where you have too much available attention for a task you are engaged in. Then the task is bound to become quickly boring due to an excess of attention, and you will be compelled toward something more pleasurable. At that point you will be good to append a supplemental, preferably pleasurable activity (like listening to music) to your current one, or seek a different and more involving activity altogether.

Monitoring your capacity for attention takes some practice, but it is something you'll likely become able to do well over time. Being aware of your attention and acting accordingly pertains to the current activity you are engaged in; it helps determine the reasons why it is unpleasurable.

Begin the Day with Low Pleasures

One of the best times you have for taking up a productive and complicated activity is shortly after you wake up. It is most common that a person wakes up in the morning in a neutral state of pleasure (experiencing no pleasure or displeasure), or even experiencing some residual pleasure from sleep. At that time, he can take up any activity that is at all pleasurable (even very slightly), since that still constitutes a gain in pleasure. If he experiences residual pleasure from having slept well, or a good mood from waking up to a gorgeous new day, he can fairly easily take up even unpleasant activities. In that case, one of the worst things he can do is default to a highly pleasurable, entertaining, and useless activity, such as watching TV or playing a videogame. Doing so, if even for just a few minutes, will set a precedent of pleasure from which it'll be extremely difficult to move on to a more demanding and less pleasurable task.

Of course the case of waking up is just a good example of a neutral (or slightly positive) state of pleasure; and starting the day with a highly pleasurable activity does not mean that the rest of that day is condemned to being entirely consumed by frivolous and highly pleasurable occupations. There are many things a person can do to restore himself to a neutral state of pleasure—such as going for a walk, or taking a shower, or having a meal, or a nap, or meditation. But it also isn't uncommon that a pleasurable activity at the beginning of the day will snowball into a whole day wasted on immoderate leisure. In any case, we can conclude it a terrible idea to *at any time* preface a productive and not too pleasurable activity with a frivolous and more pleasurable one. This often works to discourage the person from taking up his initially intended task altogether, and may lead to a whole day of procrastination.

It should also be noted that for the times when, or people who, wake up in a state of *displeasure*—their head hurts, or their bones ache, or they are feeling generally groggy—beginning the day with a productive and not very pleasurable activity is likely to be unsuccessful. Their main motivation, then, would be to get rid of their displeasure; and in that case, starting the day with a pleasurable, light-hearted activity may, on the contrary, be the best course of action—as long as it *does* relieve their displeasure, and gets them ready for a productive undertaking. (This includes watching an entertaining and stimulating video to relieve tiredness or grogginess, and taking a walk or a hot shower to relieve bodily pain.)

This method of pleasure-modulation pertains to the pleasure incentive of the activity itself in a prospective activity. It is rooted in the relativity of pleasure, which makes slightly pleasurable activities attractive to a person in a neutral—that is, a *bored*—state, but unattractive to one who's already experiencing (or has just experienced) a greater amount of pleasure from some other activity.

Using Physical Reminders

It should be clear now, that a major requirement for achieving your conscious goals, despite the unruly tides of the pleasure unconscious, is matching each of your mental states—that is, the cognitive and attention capacity you currently have, and the pleasure or displeasure you're currently feeling—with the productive tasks you are able to accomplish in those mental states. An often unforeseen obstacle to this, however, is the inadvertent failure of our memory to cooperate with us in this regard.

Most of us experience moments, when all our most urgent tasks are out of the way, and we have the time, motivation, and cognitive capacity to do something productive, but we can't think of anything we can do. Then, after squandering that opportunity on idle leisure, we remember a whole flood of low-priority tasks and obligations—such as watching a lecture, answering an email, starting a side project, or making a modest improvement in our living conditions—that we've been intending to do or neglecting for a long while.

The problem is that for most of us, and for all but a few of our most important activities, our minds won't reliably remind us of the things we've been planning to do during the moments we can actually do them. Luckily, the best solution's an extremely simple one: to set up reminders in our physical environment as a supplement to our memory. (As a quick rule, if we can assist or replace a mental task our productivity depends on with some physical instrument, it is probably a good idea.)

In this case, a whiteboard, installed in a prominent location in one's home or workplace, performs this task perfectly. By writing down everything that you want or need to do whenever it enters your consciousness—which truly requires minimal effort—you create an external memory aide that you cannot avoid looking at over the course of the day. Then, when you are at a loss for something productive to do, you can simply refer back to the whiteboard and view all the options laid out before you—which is certainly a lot easier and more effective than racking your brains over the matter. And better still, because the new scribbles on it will involuntarily catch your eye, you'll be reminded of your various short-term goals even when you don't realize you could be doing something productive—potentially converting what would've been idle leisure, into a valuable accomplishment.

It is important to make sure, however, that there is a steady turnover in the material on your whiteboard: Meaning, that you are frequently erasing old tasks (after completing them), and writing in new ones. Otherwise, if you simply fill the whiteboard with tasks you'll never erase, it will quickly become just another piece of ignored furniture—which you will fail to even notice, because of its sheer familiarity. It is, after all, novelty in your surroundings that instinctively draws your attention, while familiar things are unconsciously overlooked. To put it a different way: your whiteboard is best used for short-term tasks, and won't be too helpful for long-term, ongoing ones.

(Aside from a whiteboard, you can use sticky notes or a *to-do list* app for the same purpose. But the sticky notes may be too small to read from a distance, while the to-do list app needs to be opened from some digital device, which in itself requires effort. I think the whiteboard, which catches our eyes easily and automatically, is the best tool we have here.)

This method pertains to the overall pleasure-incentive of a prospective activity. It brings to our mind prospective activities that might already compel us enough to undertake them, but that we otherwise wouldn't have merely because we forgot about their existence.

Chapter 7

Applying What We Learned

Now we can finally return to the examples with which we began this book, and see if, with our newfound knowledge, we are now able to suggest ways to help those people out of their motivational predicaments.

The Procrastinator

Let us begin with Jim, the procrastinator. He is unable to write the paper assigned to him without leaving it to the last minute before his deadline, which causes him great stress and results in a poorer product. So, where does Jim's motivational problem lie?

The first thing that should be absolutely clear to us, is that the very act of writing his paper is anticipated as distinctly unpleasurable by Jim. His level of dread for the activity cannot be exactly determined, but we can say with full certainty that if the thought of writing the paper is not for him imbued with intense displeasure, it is at least nearly or completely devoid of all pleasure.

The negative consequences of the action *do* provide Jim with some motivation for carrying it out. But as we mentioned earlier, they don't really take hold until the last minute, and are before then more likely to cause Jim to put off writing the paper than to actually write it.

We can assume that the effort for beginning this task is miniscule, and requires nothing more than turning on a computer and opening Microsoft Word.

We will thus direct our efforts to attacking this problem on the *process* and the *consequences* front—as not much can be done to make beginning this activity any easier.

The first thing we want to know is whether there's any way to make the process of writing this paper, or rather Jim's anticipation of it, at least slightly pleasurable. For this, it's good to first address any miscellaneous factors that may cause the task to appear disproportionately more displeasurable than it really is. In this type of scenario, a person's failure to adequately imagine what he must *actually do* during the task commonly serves as such a deterrent. Very often, a person's dread before a large, seemingly insurmountable task, or his anxiety from the notion that he might be unable to do it (or do it poorly), imbue the idea of the activity with more displeasure than it physically warrants.

This can be resolved by *planning out* the activity before attempting to tackle it head on, and breaking it down into smaller, more manageable (and more imaginable) pieces. Jim can break the activity of writing his paper into a few separate parts of one section or one topic each. And this will allow him to more easily imagine what he needs to do for each one, and thus eliminate any unnecessary dread and anxiety that he may experience before the whole task but not its smaller constituents. Of course, since Jim can only write one section at a time, this won't make his job any harder, *physically* (minus, perhaps, the effort it takes him to section and plan it), but it will make his job a lot easier, *psychologically*.

Next, it is extremely important that we advise Jim not to begin his attempts at writing with any pleasurable or entertaining activities, whether to "prepare himself for writing" or some similar misguided reason, since we know that this will have precisely the opposite effect. Seeing to that, we can make additionally sure that the process of writing is not *relatively* displeasurable, by advising Jim to devote the select times when he is in a good or neutral mood expressly to writing his paper. (Keeping a whiteboard to remind him that working on the paper is an option during these times is likewise a good idea.) However, even if Jim does everything possible to make sure the activity of writing his paper does not appear displeasurable by way of relativity, it will do little good if the actual, physical process of writing it remains distinctly unpleasurable.[57]

Since we can do nothing to change the natural process of writing or the content of what Jim has to write, we have to look for auxiliary ways to make this process more pleasurable. Assuming that this will require all of Jim's attention, we cannot use music for this purpose. The best weapon Jim has here is undoubtedly caffeine, which will provide him with free pleasure that will soothe and allay the inherent displeasure he experiences from writing his assignment. Drinking coffee right before or during his attempts to write is therefore highly advisable and likely to be very effective.[58] Writing the paper alongside a friend is another great means to make the process more enjoyable; it may even make it easier if the friend makes good suggestions for what Jim should write.

Assuming that we implement all the above, it's likely that we'll

---

[57] There is, after all, a key psychological difference between switching from a neutral or unpleasant activity to a slightly pleasurable one, and switching from a highly displeasurable activity to a less unpleasant one. The former situation is agreeable since it satisfies the pleasure unconscious via a relative gain in pleasure; the latter, on the other hand, only exchanges one displeasure for another, and the pleasure unconscious, rather than being satisfied by this, will still seek to eliminate this new displeasure and exchange it for some (if only a miniscule) amount of pleasure.

[58] Positive emotions like happiness, excitement, and love can be used in the same way, but those are not reliably attainable.

still only manage to render Jim's task merely neutral in pleasure or still slightly displeasurable. But that's okay, because there's still a whole untapped source of motivation Jim can make use of in the domain of the action's consequences.

There are various ways that Jim can artificially provide *consequence* motivation for himself here. Making a bet with a friend (even a one-sided bet) is certainly a good one. Making optimistic claims or promises about finishing the paper early and then deliberately subjecting himself to his friends' scrutiny is another. He can also try *frustrating a need*—like watching TV, hanging out with friends, getting drunk, or having sex—and then incentivize himself using the satisfaction of that need as a reward for completing some fixed amount of work on his paper.

These combined motivational factors should make Jim able to work on his paper without placing himself under the axe of its due date. But if even *this* proves insufficient, then perhaps leaving it until the last minute really is the best option, since it's likely that nothing other than an impending catastrophe will be enough to motivate this person to work (at least on this particular assignment).

There's still one caveat we've yet to address, however. Assuming that Jim *does* follow our advice, and it *does* provide him with enough motivation to write his assignment without procrastinating until the very last moment, it doesn't automatically follow that he will make any meaningful progress on it. It is possible, indeed even likely, that shortly after beginning, Jim will switch from writing the paper to a more pleasurable task, and then be totally unable to resume his work. It is one thing to start a task and another to persist at that task without quitting after just five or ten minutes. But we know exactly how to address this problem.

Here we have the quintessential problem of modulating a person's motivation so that he refrains from swapping his current activity for a more pleasurable prospective one. We already know that this is a matter of having the pleasure of one's present activity plus the consequences of quitting it outweigh the pleasure-incentive of all three dimensions—the activation energy, the act, and the result—of the prospective activity (refer to *Figure 3* above). Since we've already done everything we could to make the current activity as pleasurable as possible, and its consequences as significant as possible, our only remaining option is to cut down the promise of pleasure contained in every other activity. Fortunately, this doesn't require Jim to perform the same kind of motivational manipulations detailed above to literally *every* activity more pleasurable than writing his paper. All he needs is to *seclude himself* from those activities.

What will enable Jim to persist at his task without swapping it for a more pleasurable one, is simply keeping all such activities out of his reach, so that the effort now needed to begin those activities makes doing so an unattractive prospect. Working in a setting devoid of any opportunities for those activities—a library or a basement, for instance—is the standard, potent way of accomplishing this. But this doesn't have to go nearly as far as complete seclusion: Often something as simple as unplugging one's TV or internet creates enough of an effort-barrier to prevent a person from abandoning his work for those activities.

With that, we can close the book on Jim. If he follows our advice, he will be very likely to succeed. And that is the best we can do for him.

The Gym Goer

Let's now turn our attention to Annemarie, who cannot find the motivation to go to the gym and work out.

Annemarie's situation encounters motivational problems on all three fronts. First, just making her way to the gym requires that she leaves her house and travels some distance to get there. We do not know exactly how far she has to travel, but in any case it undoubtedly requires a non-negligible amount of effort. Second, the process of working out is itself bound to be, at least partially, displeasurable, since it certainly causes physical pain, and is likely to be monotonous as well. And third, the consequences of actually working out are no longer concrete for Annemarie. We can assume that in the first several weeks, when she diligently attended the gym every day, she was mostly motivated by the desired *consequences* of doing so. But after not seeing much significant results after that time, those consequences ceased seeming real to her and transitioned into more of an abstract, possibly unreachable goal. Essentially, she lost that aspect of her motivation.

Plus, it's also likely that the *physical activity* of working out became more monotonous and displeasurable for her over time.[59]

Because the effort Annemarie must exert to get to the gym is an issue of distance, she can't do much to reduce the actual amount of *effort* that action requires. She can, nevertheless, find ways to reduce its *displeasure*. Listening to music or an audiobook while walking to the gym is a great, standard way to make that walk more enjoyable—and making the trip with a friend will yield the same effect. Another thing Annemarie can do is use the opportunity to go to the gym when she's already made the journey there for another reason (like when she's passing by the gym on her way back from her friend's house) or when she has more than one reason for making that journey (like to buy groceries at a good supermarket next to her gym).

(Because hers isn't a one-and-done task, however, but something she has to do on an ongoing basis, jotting it down on a whiteboard will likely prove ineffective—as she'll simply get used to this written reminder, and soon cease to notice it.)

To make the actual process of working out more pleasurable, Annemarie can utilize much of the same resources.

---

[59] In fact, the very thought of working toward a goal contributes to the pleasure a person derives from an activity, imbuing it with excitement and purpose; while thinking about that same activity as a kind of obligation, which has to be performed for some abstract and tenuous reasons, is apt to have the exact opposite effect.

Listening to music while working out would certainly help make the process more enjoyable, but there's a good chance this alone won't be sufficient to make the activity pleasurable as a whole. Listening to an audiobook might do the trick, but since that usually requires a person's undivided attention, it's more likely to distract Annemarie from the actual process of working out, and cause her to do so only halfheartedly. Working out with a friend is probably the best option here. Adding a social aspect to the activity will go a long way to making it enjoyable without producing any drain on actual performance. Another option is taking one of the many workout supplements on the market today, which are essentially drugs that provide free chemical pleasure (and possibly even inhibit some physical pain), in order to tackle the monotony and physical discomfort of working out. However, I do not know how advisable such products are for one's long term health.

While it is doubtful whether we can do anything to restore Annemarie's original eagerness for the results of working out—at least until she sees significant results from doing so—we can still supply her consequence motivation from elsewhere. If she's already taken our advice and works out with a friend, that itself is a fruitful source of consequence motivation: Then, failing to go to the gym also becomes letting her friend down, which may be further enhanced with feelings of guilt and embarrassment if she doesn't want to appear lazy or pathetic in front of that friend. Getting a personal trainer is another great option, perhaps if Annemarie is unable to find a friend to frequent the gym with her, or if that friend doesn't provide enough motivation on his or her own. A personal trainer serves essentially the same motivating role as a gym buddy, only with greater intensity, since they tend to be angrier and judge more critically than just some miscellaneous friend. [60]

---

[60] The advice on technique and fitness regimen that a personal trainer provides can also be quite invaluable, including the additional

And, of course, Annemarie can also make a wager with someone that she'll attend the gym; which is always a good source of additional consequence motivation.

Once Annemarie amasses enough motivation to go to the gym, we don't need to worry much about preventing her from quitting her workout and switching to a more pleasurable activity. For one thing, the gym is a fairly secluded place, and all such activities are likely far out of her reach. Additionally, if she attends the gym with a friend or personal trainer, simply quitting in the middle of a workout is a very unsavory option, since she will have to incur a good amount of negative emotion (whether it be embarrassment, or anxiety, or shame) if she leaves without notifying them, or from having to explain herself before them.

I think that covers all the issues in this scenario. And with that, we can do no more here.

The Smoker

John, the smoker, is a particularly interesting case. The majority of people are likely to think that his situation is fundamentally different from our other examples, since his addiction to cigarettes is (at least in part) physical, while the problems in our other cases seem to be entirely psychological. We, who are now aware of the true nature of motivation, should know that this distinction is superficial.

A person who is said to be *psychologically* addicted to a substance or activity consistently seeks it out from a want of pleasure. A person who is said to be *physically* addicted (to what is nearly always a substance) seeks that substance because he experiences some type of displeasure, usually from chemical influences, when he is without it. This distinction is, of course, a valid one. But in the end, it all boils down to the common currency of pleasure and displeasure, and we can use our tools

---

benefit of a planned course of action, plus an imaginable layout of the results one can expect after a given period of time.

for controlling motivation to battle both.

We've already seen John apply our methods to the *starting* aspect of his undesired activity, by making it physically harder for himself to begin the act of smoking. He did just about everything he could to make the task of obtaining a cigarette as difficult as possible. But while this was certainly a commendable attempt, it proved to be insufficient.

So, where did John lack motivation? It wasn't in the effort necessary to begin smoking, since he dealt with that. His consequence motivation didn't seem to be lacking either, since it prevented him from smoking for as long as he did. The actual act of smoking was certainly very alluring for him in the pleasure it promised to give and the displeasure it promised to relieve, but the effort needed to start it and the thoughts of its negative consequences seemed to keep the impulse at bay. John's attempt to quit fell apart when the displeasure from not smoking and his desire to smoke prevented him from doing his work, adding very substantial negative consequences to *not* smoking. This tipped the scales, and John finally succumbed.

The first and rather obvious step in improving John's situation, then, is removing those negative consequences of sticking with his resolution to quit. We would advise him to take some time off of work, and devote that time to leisure, so that his struggle against smoking will not distract him from anything important. This should accomplish reducing John's problem to merely that of refraining from a powerful impulse to seek pleasure (in smoking) and reduce displeasure (from lack of nicotine), without having to deal with other problems besides. But even then, there is still the risk that that impulse will grow too strong, and John won't be able to resist it despite all the effort he must exert to gratify it, and all the detrimental consequences that will come of it.

There is, of course, room to make obtaining a cigarette *even more* difficult, and increase the consequences of smoking even further; but this will likely have sharply diminishing benefits. Probably the best thing that can be done is to put John in an environment completely devoid of cigarettes, where obtaining one would be physically impossible; but something like that is usually unfeasible. Excluding that option, the second best approach is to have John engage in some other activities that bring pleasure.

John's urge to smoke consists of a want for pleasure, which can be satisfied by various means, and a desire to reduce the displeasure from his lack of nicotine, which can be satisfied only by cigarettes or some other source of the chemical. The first part of his compulsion to smoke can be satiated by replacing the act of smoking with something else that brings pleasure—listening to music, or going for a hike or a swim, or drinking a smoothie, or watching TV, or even ingesting some other chemical (like caffeine).[61] Primarily, this will serve to allay his want for pleasure from his usual source (the cigarette). But it will also have the peripheral benefit of soothing the second part of John's compulsion (the displeasure), by making his current activity more pleasurable, and thus the prospective activity of smoking relatively less so. Just as a mother's caress makes a sick child feel better because it is pleasurable, and takes his attention away from the pain of his sickness; so will doing something pleasurable cushion the displeasure John feels from an absence of nicotine, and make his compulsion to relieve it by smoking much less feverishly desired than if it was the sole thing he was experiencing.

---

[61] There is, however, an important danger one must avoid here. The act of smoking becomes associatively linked in a person's mind with other activities before, during, or after which he would typically smoke. As a result, engaging in those activities will trigger in him a powerful urge for a cigarette; and in his attempts at quitting, he should never try to replace smoking with any of these, as they will only amplify his cravings. Most smokers, for example, consume coffee in conjunction with cigarettes—making it a decidedly bad idea for them to try and replace smoking with caffeine. It is therefore best to replace cigarettes with an entirely fresh, new, and pleasurable activity, ideally one that the person has never tried before.

If John does not want to take a replacement nicotine substance like gum or the patch, we have no additional advice left to give him. He can do nothing to relieve his displeasure and must instead bear it, withholding all the while from his urges to smoke. And if he adheres to our advice and succeeds in resisting it, the displeasure will soon lessen and eventually fade away altogether.[62] It is important to realize that it is precisely

---

[62] If John does choose to make use of alternative sources of nicotine, the methods outlined here will still be entirely valid, and provide supplementary help in his attempts at quitting. It's also useful to note, that the replacement sources of nicotine shouldn't be used to replace smoking altogether, but instead be a way to wean the person off the drug by taking smaller and smaller doses of it. This'll be a good method if each successive nicotine patch or piece of gum has less nicotine in it then the last, since that will allow the person to spread out a lot of displeasure over time into many portions of a much slighter displeasure, which will certainly make it easier to deal with. However, doing the same thing with cigarettes, and smoking less and less of them on each successive day, isn't something I'd recommend; since this leaves the option of smoking more than one's allotted amount each day to one's own private discretion. It's easy to simply put another cigarette in one's mouth when they are at hand, but not quite so to put on a second nicotine patch. If cigarettes are your only weapon, it's much better to quit cold turkey, as recommended here, than to gradually attempt to wean yourself off of them.

(2017 Addition): Since writing this book in 2013, a new technology has emerged to make quitting a lot easier: Vaporizers. These are essentially sophisticated electronic-cigarettes, which use a heating element (a metal coil of wire with electricity running through it) to turn a special liquid formula (an inert solvent, with nicotine and flavorings dissolved in it) into an inhalable vapor, which the person then breathes as a substitute for cigarette smoke. The strategy for using these "vapes" to quit smoking is pretty much identical to that of using the nicotine patch or the gum. The person starts with a liquid containing a high nicotine content, and gradually switches to one with less and less nicotine, until he is vaping a liquid with no nicotine whatsoever. These devices are incredibly effective, and have helped millions of people quit cigarettes in an extremely short

because the urge to smoke *does* lessen with time (if it is not indulged) that makes quitting an attainable possibility. If it instead grew stronger with time when neglected, such as the sexual urge, all attempts to banish it would be fruitless, and a great deal of effort would need to be spent merely to resist it.[63]

The urge for a cigarette, however, most certainly does come back, and specifically as the result of having one. Many former smokers who haven't had a cigarette (or even wanted one) for months or years, find their former cravings return with full force—and themselves relapsing into addiction—after inadvertently smoking only a single cigarette.

The solution, of course, is after having quit smoking, to stick with it; and to avoid having another cigarette, *ever*, if one wants to avoid a relapse. This can, like everything else, be accomplished using the motivational techniques listed above—the most potent of which is to make obtaining a cigarette as difficult for oneself as possible (which means never buying a pack, and certainly never having any at hand to smoke when one wishes).

The Video Gamer

Junseo the video gamer is completely entranced by his

---

amount of time; which should make perfect sense to us, since they provide both the nicotine *and* the physical pleasure that comes with the act of smoking—being both fun to use, and coming in hundreds of tasty flavors (unlike the gum, which can taste nasty; or the patch, which is pleasure-neutral).

There is, however, one important pitfall to avoid when using a vaporizer to quit smoking. And that is to have a physical cigarette or two *in addition* to using the vape. Vaping does not eliminate the urge for a cigarette; it is something one has to do *instead* of smoking, until one's urge for a traditional cigarette goes away. It can't be successfully used *in conjunction* with cigarettes, which usually leads to smoking twice as much.

[63] Attempting to do so for sex, of course, can and does lead to acute psychological illness.

videogame and is hardly able to do anything else other than play it. We may say that he exhibits a quintessential psychological addiction to the game (since it is the compulsion to seek pleasure that draws him to it), except for the fact that this *addiction* lasts for only six days. But then, the only reason Junseo was able to quit the game after only six days was that, in those six days, he managed to finish the game. After that, the game ceased to hold the same excitement for him, since it no longer provided any goals to reach or any promise for future, novel gameplay.

With what we now know about motivation, we can confidently predict that if Junseo's game took twelve days (or even thirty days) to beat instead of six, then *that* would be how long he would consequently play it, and how long his *addiction* to it would last.[64] If the game could continue indefinitely without a set end, or if there was a multitude of similarly exciting games easily available for Junseo to play after he beat this one, it's quite possible that his addiction to this game, or to games in general, would continue indefinitely as well.[65]

In any case, we cannot help but consider it very peculiar that simply being exposed for a short time to a videogame is enough for Junseo to contract a powerful psychological addiction to it, even if only for six days. But we must now recognize how superficial the term addiction, especially *psychological addiction,* really is. After all, the roots of Junseo's temporary addiction are entirely known to us: It is rooted in the ubiquitous need for pleasure biologically imbued in all persons. In fact, we can justly say that all human beings are by

---

[64] There are a multitude of similar cases in which a transient addiction to a videogame lasts for this kind of time period, and even greater ones, ending only when the person finally grows bored of the game (whether due to beating it or otherwise).

[65] That is, at least until he experiences a powerful psychological revulsion—a shameful or guilty conscience—from his addiction; or until he undergoes a major change in circumstances, whether of his own accord or otherwise, that prevents him from gaming.

their nature addicts: addicts to pleasure. It is only when that pleasure is predominantly acquired from a single, unhealthy source—as Junseo's is from videogames—that we conventionally label it an *addiction*.

Junseo's motivational problem is clearly that playing the game, for him, is simply too damn enjoyable.

We have already mentioned earlier in this book the way a videogame addiction like this can be overcome by storing the game several miles away, committing the person to go through great efforts to start playing it. This is perfectly valid in Junseo's case too, and doing something like that is almost certainly the best alternative he has for quitting it. Of course, Junseo does eventually quit the game because he beats it. That is another effective way to quit an addictive videogame, only it requires the greatest amount of wasted time and effort before it's achieved.

I only want to add one additional technique that can be implemented in this situation. It is to delete the saved file and start the game anew after already completing a good portion of it (maybe a quarter of it, maybe half, maybe 75%). Then, the prospect of playing the game no longer becomes a purely pleasurable one, since getting to the exciting, novel parts of the game (the ones that have not been reached yet) now requires replaying the earlier parts that are no longer new or interesting. The dread of the boring rote repetition of the first parts of the game, which may take hours or days to get through, is likely to be enough to overpower the excitement and novelty promised by the later parts. Additionally, the knowledge of having deliberately deleted the game file in order to prevent himself from playing it will have plenty of opportunity to rouse a feeling of shame and/or guilt in the person (also deterring him from the game or causing him to quit in the middle of it) if he does succumb and decides to start it anew.

It is also important to note that completing a game often leads people to seek pleasure in another, similar game. After all, their impulse to seek pleasure is still there, only now this particular game provides no prospect of satisfying it. The result is that this played-out game will no longer occupy the person's mind, and all his motivation for seeking a similar type of enjoyment becomes free for finding other games that provide the same satisfaction—and since the motivation for acquiring that pleasure is powerful, because that first game was so enjoyable, he will be willing to invest a massive amount of effort to find a replacement, and very likely succeed in doing so. If that first game is abridged halfway, however, the motivational landscape will be quite different. [66] That first game will still occupy the person's mind as a way to satisfy his yearning for enjoyment, but he will be held back from it by the aforementioned disincentives. Then, the prospects of finding a new game and restarting the old one will compel the person more or less equally. [67] And he will be much more likely to choose neither.

In this way, constraining himself to start a partially completed game all over again, if he wants to play it, effectively inoculates the person against such games altogether. Storing the game where it cannot be easily reached will also have the same effect. Both, after all, provide a very similar impediment

---

[66] I find it useful, in thinking about motivation, to imagine all the pleasurable activities available to a person as hills scattered around an otherwise flat landscape, with the person standing at its center. The height of each hill is proportional to the pleasure the activity it stands for will bring, and the distance of the person from each hill represents how difficult that activity is to begin. The person will of course want to climb the hills, and be drawn to their peaks.

Picturing all the activities a person is drawn to for pleasure and how easy it is for him to begin them in this kind of '*motivational landscape*' can make quickly apparent which activities he will most strongly gravitate to when he's bored, and the best ways this can be altered (that is, by cutting down some of the hills or by moving them further away).

[67] His thoughts may be somewhere along the lines of: "If I were to find a new game, I might as well restart and finish the old one since that is what I really want."

to playing the game. In each case, the person must do something time consuming, effortful, and boring in order to resume playing the game from where it is interesting for him. Those are the best, most effective techniques for dealing with this kind of situation. But peripheral sources of motivation are, as always, a helpful supplement to one's primary efforts.

The Sleeper

We finally arrive at our last example: Tom, the sleeper. Tom's case differs from the preceding ones in that, rather than battling against a strong compulsion toward a peculiar behavior while trying to do its opposite, he is imperceptibly eased by motivational forces in his environment to default in excess to one of the most basic biological functions: sleep.

To be able to understand Tom's case, we must first abandon the primitive notion that a person's sleep is determined by a psychologically independent biological clock, which is set to somewhere between seven and eight hours each day; and anybody who consistently sleeps longer or shorter than that must be afflicted with some kind of psychological or biological malady. Sleep is a behavior like any other, and it is subject to all the same principles of motivation and of the pleasure unconscious. After all, is sleep not pleasurable? Does it not relieve tiredness, which is displeasurable?

Sleep *is* pleasurable, even without the aspect of tiredness. But let's first examine the psychology of tiredness, to see whether *that* might be responsible for Tom's excessive sleeping.[68]

What most people don't realize, is that the feeling of tiredness isn't just the result of staying awake for a full day. Rather, it is a very distinct psychological phenomenon, set off

---

[68] The following analysis of the dynamics of tiredness, and the psychology underlying it, was first added in 2017—after I realized that *this*, more than any other factor, was actually the primary (if not the sole) cause behind the majority of cases of oversleeping.

by a very specific psychological trigger—and that trigger is: forcing oneself to pay attention to something that is entirely boring, unpleasurable, or monotonous. As we already know, the pleasure unconscious will strive to pull your attention away from precisely such things; but you'll often have some other source of motivation—usually consequence motivation—that keeps your attention fixed on it. It is this internal struggle to focus your attention on something that repels it—that is, to willfully bear boredom, without seeking escape into something pleasurable—that will naturally produce the sensation of tiredness.

Let's say you are reading a book, which has just entered a boring stretch, but you force yourself to keep reading in order to get to another exciting part—well, this is going to make you extremely tired. Let's say you are at a lecture, and the professor is droning on languidly, but you make yourself listen anyway because that material will be on the test—you will likely fall asleep in your seat. (I have often observed as much as half of a fully packed and well-rested auditorium fall dead asleep at an especially boring lecture.) Or let's say you are inside a hypnotist's office, watching his gold pocket watch swing monotonously in front of your face, but you can't look away or else this intimidating man will scold you for taking your eyes off of it—you will, precisely as he intended, grow incredibly tired. (By the same effect, on a recent whale-watching cruise I went on, I witnessed nearly the whole boat of sixty well-rested tourists completely asleep after an hour or so of staring intently at the monotonously swaying ocean, waiting to see a small humpback whale that surfaced every five or ten minutes.) It is this little-recognized facet of the human mind that hypnotists secretly make use of—by giving a hollow, substance-less speech in a slow, monotonous voice; by getting people to focus on the rhythmical movement, or the complete stillness, of an inanimate object; or by making them perform some mindless, tedious task, like counting all the way down from fifty—to induce an intense tiredness.

And this very same thing may be responsible for Tom's

oversleeping. If a central part of Tom's daily routine is making him tired in the above manner, it is virtually guaranteed he'll be sleeping more than he should. A likely candidate for this is Tom's job. As we already know, the enjoyment a person receives from an activity greatly depends on his ability to engage in it. And when his attention capacity decreases over the course of a day, for any reason, so will his ability to engage in a mentally demanding task. Given that Tom works from home at his computer, he could very well be forcing himself to continue working, even after his attention capacity can no longer handle it, and the process becomes boring and intractable. This will surely make him grow very tired; and the harder he struggles, the more tired he will get. There is nothing so psychologically exhausting as trying to successfully carry out an intellectual task which has become, at least for the moment, too mentally difficult.[69]

People who hold a nine-to-five office job, it should be noted, also experience tiredness under the same conditions. But since they have no ready opportunity to fall asleep at their office, they naturally find other ways to deal with getting tired at work (usually by means of coffee), and make it to the end of their workdays in a more or less productive fashion. (Or, if they are given a task they must complete by a deadline, it is their anxiety that'll motivate them to stay awake.)

Tom, on the other hand, working as he does a mere stone's throw away from his bed, and being free to set his own schedule, has zero impediments to satisfying his tiredness with sleep—and can therefore piece out his work in several hour portions, in between catnaps, and not even notice the extra time being whittled away by his slumber. (I personally experienced something like this when I decided, one time, to do nothing but read *Les Misérables* all day, every day, until I finally finished the book. I had to abandon this experiment

---

[69] And this makes perfect evolutionary sense. It is sleep, after all, that rejuvenates one's attention capacity, and thus restores one's ability to engage in a mentally demanding task.

after two or three days, however, because I suddenly found myself sleeping almost fourteen hours per diem. The book simply couldn't hold my interest for more than several hours at a stretch, and when I attempted to carry on past that, I was unable to resist the overpowering pull toward slumber.) If this is the case with Tom and his job, or if tiredness from some other source is a big driving force of his oversleeping—whether that tiredness is caused by his work, his leisure, or his eating habits (and we know overeating is a common cause of tiredness, at least in part because it restricts one's attention capacity by diverting blood flow away from the brain)—we'd have to advise Tom to begin observing the things that are making him tired, and to either stop doing them the moment they become unpleasurable, make them more pleasurable by means of the motivational techniques listed above, or simply leave his house whenever he begins feeling tired, so that he doesn't have the option to return back to his bed.[70]

---

[70] In addition to this, Tom would be good to also take note of two other types of—purely physical—tiredness: (1) tiredness of the body, and (2) tiredness of the eyes. Like the first type of tiredness, which we may call tiredness of the mind, each produces a distinct sensation of displeasure, which is best relieved by sleeping, and is therefore a strong motivator towards sleep. Tiredness of the body is caused by an overexertion of one's muscles—any muscles—causing them to ache with additional movement, and motivating the person to stay still and rest, which frequently leads to sleep. (This is unlikely to be the problem in Tom's case, since he spends the majority of his time at home. But if he does overexert himself whenever he visits the gym, it might be a contributing factor to his oversleeping. In this case, we'd have to advise Tom to take it easier, or to only do so at the end of the day, right before he would naturally go to sleep.) The next type of physical tiredness, tiredness of the eyes, is the result of overworking or straining them—by a prolonged exposure to bright light (such as from the sun or a computer screen), by engaging in optically strenuous tasks (such as reading very small print or without one's proper prescription of glasses), or simply by using one's eyes in

But Tom's sedentary lifestyle needs not include any of those somniferous factors, which essentially hypnotize him to sleep without his knowing it, in order to result in him slumbering eleven hours a day. The sheer fact that sleep is pleasurable all on its own, without tiredness having to play a part, is more than enough to cause Tom to overindulge in it—that is, as a way to obtain pleasure, as opposed to relieve displeasure. And, in the absence of any significant sources of tiredness, we can assume *this* to be Tom's main motivation for defaulting to it so frequently.

From just one look at Tom's motivational landscape, we can see what conditions would coax him to favor sleep over just about all other pleasurable activities. The biggest problem Tom undeniably has is that sleep is just too easily accessible for him. In the whole time he spends in his apartment, which seems to be the lion's share of each day, his bed stands right alongside him, and he constantly has the option to quit whatever he's doing and bury himself in it instead. And doing so requires virtually no effort on Tom's part; which means, it's an activity completely devoid of activation energy.

So, we know that for Tom the activity of sleep is pleasurable, requires no effort to begin, and is almost always available. That alone, however, will not sentence him to engage

---

their regular manner over the course of a long day. The aftermath is a burning or painful sensation in one's eyes, or a heaviness of one's eyelids, that makes a person want nothing more than to lay back and *rest his eyes*, which almost invariably leads to sleep. (This could very well be a major cause of Tom's tiredness. But if so, it would be extremely noticeable and easily fixable—like by obtaining a new pair of glasses, putting curtains on his windows, or dimming down his computer screen.) Hypnotists make ample use of these types of tiredness as well—like when they instruct their subjects to lift up an arm and hold it raised high for a few minutes; or to focus their eyes on something that's not directly in front of them, tracking it only with their eyeballs, while their heads remain perfectly still (this too produces an immense strain on the eyes). [End of the 2017 addition.]

in it for those three extra hours each day. Indeed, there is a substantial amount of people who live in the same conditions and do not fall into this same behavior. The difference lies, assuming that tiredness isn't the main culprit, in Tom's consequence motivation. That is the one motivational aspect of the activity of sleep, in Tom's case, that we've yet to consider. And we can quickly see that it too rules in the favor of sleep rather than against it.

First off, we know that even after accounting for Tom's extra hours of sleep, he still has plenty of time to meet all his obligations, engage in miscellaneous leisure, and have a fair amount of idle time remaining. Thus, there are no physical consequences for Tom's superfluous sleep, nothing that will crash down upon him or hurt him for it, nothing to cause him anxiety that would prevent him from sleeping or wrench him out of his bed. Tom may feel a tinge of shame for killing that extra time sleeping—after all, he does consciously disapprove of the situation—but that clearly doesn't provide enough negative affect to overcome the physical pleasure that sleep brings him.

The only significant consequence motivation Tom has against sleeping is its opportunity cost: the things he could be investing his time in instead of sleep. It does not seem that Tom has many activities that he is passionate or excited about and that he values a lot more highly than sleep. But even if he did, there is the unavoidable fact that all such activities would require a significantly greater amount of effort, or activation energy, than retiring to his bed. Engaging in them would require traveling, leaving the house, exerting some other miscellaneous effort, while plopping into bed will continue to require only that, and be—in at least that respect—the more attractive alternative. For that reason, as long as sleep remains the easiest pleasurable activity Tom has available to him, it will continue to have a powerful foothold in his life.

So, how would we remedy this situation? We want Tom to choose sleep less often, and to wake up from it sooner when he does. Well, our first option is to make the *physical* process of sleep less pleasurable—like by replacing Tom's mattress with a thin matt on the bare floor; or replacing his sheets with coarse, tickling, or malodorous ones; or substituting his pillows with harder, smaller, less comfortable ones; or maybe doing away with his pillows altogether. Although this could work in extreme cases, its drawbacks can easily outweigh its benefits. A less comfortable bed might cause Tom to get a less restful night's sleep, which might actually result in his sleeping more rather than less. (In fact, not getting a restful enough sleep—whether for physical, mental, or biological reasons—may very well be the cause of Tom's oversleeping in the first place.)

Our second option is making the preliminary act of *getting in bed* require more effort. We can, for example, advise Tom to fill his bed with clutter, so he must invest the time to clean it off before lying down; or we can advise him to place his bed on a top bunk, so he would have to climb to get in it. But filling his bed with clutter every morning would itself require effort; and if we make climbing *into* his bed more difficult, it would also make it more difficult for him to climb out. No, our best solution here is making a drastic change to Tom's living situation.

Rather than getting Tom to spend less time specifically in his bed, we can achieve the same results if we, more generally, get Tom to spend less time in his apartment. The fundamental method, however, remains the same: To render Tom's house less pleasurable to be in. One gargantuan problem Tom has is that a lot of the pleasures he seeks other than sleep are to be found in his bed as well: We've already noted that he spends much of his leisure hours reading and watching TV in his bed. The dreadful effect is that these activities segue directly into sleep, since—when he becomes bored of them—sleep is the easiest, most available, and most pleasurable option he has. Removing such pleasures from Tom's house should then cause him to seek his enjoyment elsewhere, and thus not allow him to default to his bed quite so easily. The less amenable Tom's apartment is to satisfying his pleasure unconscious, the more likely he will be to spend his time outside it.[71]

Once we successfully get rid of Tom's TV, his books (or at least the lighting he has for reading them), as well as whatever other easily available pleasures there are in his house, the solitary activity of sleep will cease being such an attractive prospect for him, since—in the absence of all those other pleasurable activities easing him into it—the pleasure it's able to bring him is really quite miniscule. His sleeping will then be placed *in opposition* to those highly pleasurable activities, and he'll be forced to choose between *them* and *it*, as opposed to the two dovetailing into each other. Whether or not this is enough to get Tom out of his house, however, a great piece of advice we can give him—under any circumstances—is to not work where he sleeps.

Even if Tom doesn't have to, leaving his apartment to work from some office or library would serve him well in keeping him away from his bed for a large chunk of the day. It would be better still if that office was a substantial distance from where he lives, making it too daunting a proposition to return home for a quick nap. Taking on other obligations that get him out of the house would have a similar effect. Signing up for some kind of class, for example, and paying in advanced

---

[71] (2017 Addition): Another factor, which I knew nothing about when I first wrote this, is that the very posture of lying down—that is, of being horizontal—exerts a unique psychological influence on a person's mind, genuinely predisposing him to grow tired, close his eyes, and drift off to sleep, in a way that sitting, standing, or walking around never does. If you're reading a boring book while lying in bed, for instance, you'll be *very intensely* hypnotized into slumber; but if you're reading that book sitting at your desk, the hypnotic effect will be much weaker. (If you are reading the book standing up, of course, this effect will be weaker still; and it will be much weaker than that if you do so while walking around.) The key piece of advice here is to avoid doing boring, effortful, or unpleasurable activities (or those that may become boring, effortful, or unpleasurable) while lying in one's bed—period.

so that he doesn't have the option to bow out, would certainly work well in achieving this.

It may also prove helpful if Tom moves out of his apartment altogether, and into different living quarters—preferably with roommates or a girlfriend. This would have the double benefit of making his behavior subject to the scrutiny of others, and providing him with a readily available source of people, which he can spend enjoyable time with outside of his bed—even if still in his home.

With that, we may be sure of having given Tom the best advice we could; and can now close the book on his case, and round out this chapter.[72]

---

[72] There are, of course, other factors that we neglected to consider about Tom's affinity for sleep. It is certainly true that chronically sleeping in excess, as Tom does, most often only makes the person more tired rather than less, and causes him to sleep that same amount the next day, and the next, in a self-perpetuating cycle. We may think, then, that forcibly breaking this cycle by sleeping only a regular amount for several days would remedy Tom's situation. While this is true, it won't do much good if the conditions that led Tom to initiate that cycle in the first place remain the same—once he succeeds in breaking that cycle, his situation will inevitably coax him once more into sleeping those extra few hours, beginning the cycle all over again.

It may also be possible that Tom, by sheer virtue of his genetic disposition, rather than any extraneous factors in his environment, naturally experiences a more intense tiredness than the average person. Of course this would, by the principles of the pleasure unconscious, cause him to sleep more than most others. In that case, managing it would be a matter of making certain that the other negative affects that compete with his tiredness—such as anxiety about going to work or meeting other obligations—be more intense than it is, and also present most of the time. But even then, as soon as those obligations lax, Tom would once again be drawn into taking an excessive amount of sleep. If it really *is* a matter of genetics, it's pretty much unavoidable that Tom will simply be someone who must sleep longer than the average person. (Coffee might help.)

Conclusion

I hope that, having finished this book, the reader has gained a valuable understanding of the motivational forces at play in his or her own life, and will be able—in the future—to apply the methods we detailed here, and the advice we gave to our five subjects, to his or her own situation. But these methods are, of course, only bandages, crutches in the areas of our lives where we lack intense passion that extends far beyond the act itself and into a truly important and passion-filled aspect of our lives.[73]

We must always seek to find our calling in life, something that fills us with passion and excitement. Nothing can rival the motivation a person derives from something that he both enjoys and profits from. And the greatest times are the ones in which our goals and motivations seamlessly align, when we are effortlessly propelled forward and can do no wrong.

But such things are hard to find; and even upon finding them, it is inevitable that they too will yield their own problems and moments of demotivation. Even the hungriest, most driven and motivated man will find areas and times in his life where his motivation is insufficient or absent, and where he can derive great benefit from our methods.

It is best to follow our passions, to find the things that we love and never stop pursuing them. But life will always have its snags and its hurdles, and what we cannot reach flying, we must reach limping.

---

[73] A person passionate about a subject and eager to express his views will find no problem writing a paper on it (especially on his own terms), and a person powerfully driven to excel at martial arts will not be paralyzed before the notion of going to the gym.